A Maze In Greece

Jess Harpur

easyBroom

A Maze In Greece

An easyBroom book

Copyright © 2014 Jess Harpur

ISBN 978-0-9576288-2-3

The right of Jess Harpur to be identified as the author of this work has been asserted in accordance with Sections 77 and 78 of the Copyright, Designs and Patents Act 1988

Illustrations and Cover Design: Jess Harpur

A catalogue record of this book is available from The British Library

**For all those who have asked
"Are we there yet?"**

Contents

Chapter 1 • Imagine

Imagine you are born in a maze. As you grow up, your family and the other people you come into contact with, don't give any indication that it's a maze, or even that there is anything at all unusual about your surroundings. Their behaviour gives you no hint whatsoever that you are living in anything other than a completely normal, natural environment, and consequently you don't give it any thought. With no knowledge that you are living in a maze, there is no reason to look for a way out, nor even any reason to think there is one. You learn to assimilate by following the example of your family and their associates.

As time passes, you notice that there are some avenues down which neither your family nor anyone else ever goes (with the exception of some of the Elders, and a few strangers). Your natural curiosity prompts you to ask what is down those avenues.

Your family replies that those avenues must be avoided at all costs because unimaginable horrors lie in wait for those foolish enough to explore them. They tell you of people who ignored this good advice who have never been heard of again.

You ponder this for a while, then mention that you've seen some of the Elders, and also some strangers, going in and out of those avenues. Your family says, "The Elders have a special power to protect them."

"But what about the strangers?" you ask.

"That's why they are called strangers," they reply. "Stay clear of strangers because they are agents of the evil powers that lurk in the dark corners of those avenues."

Your curiosity remains, but the fear of the unknown

1

evil that awaits any exploration of those tempting avenues keeps your natural inquisitiveness in check, and you make do with exploring the other parts of your local habitat. In your travels, you sometimes see one or other of the Groundsmen, who work for the Elders, setting up diversions here and there. You enquire what they are for, and they cheerfully respond that it's nothing to worry about, just routine maintenance. You obediently follow the diversions, but after a while, you come to realise that no matter what route you take your explorations always lead you back to the centre. One day, although you always try not to get too close to them, you overhear some strangers talking, and one of them says, "It's just like a maze, really."

You ask your family what a 'maze' is. You notice that they look at each other for a moment, and then they encourage you to talk to one of the Elders, who, they remind you, are always happy to offer guidance.

The Elders are figures of authority, custodians of the law, teachers, and arbiters of moral judgement, whose self-confidence, combined with the deference everyone shows them, makes approaching them a serious undertaking. However, you follow your family's advice, and locating an Elder you ask, "Please, can you tell me, what is a maze?"

The Elder smiles benevolently at you for a while, making you wonder if perhaps you shouldn't have asked the question, and then replies, "When is a maze not a maze? ... when it's amazing!"

The Elder's response is not what you expected, and you are not sure if he was serious or joking. You don't know what do. If it was a joke and you don't laugh it will be disrespectful, but it will also be disrespectful if you do laugh and it was a serious answer. The Elder's expression gives you no clue. Embarrassed, you look over your shoulder, make a noise in your throat which you hope will be interpreted as the correct response and say, "ah...I see," further hoping you'll be let off the hook.

However, despite your embarrassment you still want to ask the Elder about what he said, but before you can compose your words he has patted you on your head, smiled that benevolent smile again while raising an eyebrow (which you interpret to mean, "you aren't foolish enough to pursue this, are you?") and has turned to walk away. You are left thinking that whether he was joking or serious, it wasn't a proper answer to your question, despite the reference to a 'maze'. But you also know beyond any doubt that Elders must be shown the utmost respect, so you feel you have no choice but to accept his words.

When you get home, your family ask what the Elder said. When you tell them, they smile and clap their hands with obvious delight, and say, "See! We told you they would give you guidance!"

In the face of their overwhelming joy you feel you must suppress your feelings of dissatisfaction, of having been tricked, and smile with them - because the Elders say it is very bad to cause your family pain. Consequently, you do your best to appear to be as joyous as they are, even though you know you are acting falsely, and acting falsely is something the Elders also say is very bad.

A small knot of confusion establishes itself in your brain as you try to resolve this conflict. Unable to do so, you turn your attention to the Elder's words. And the knot grows bigger, and tighter. The truth is you think it was a silly answer that wasn't a proper answer at all, just a 'clever' playing with words, but you feel guilty for thinking it because the Elders are wise, and your family thought it was brilliant. You wonder if perhaps you lack the ability to appreciate the profundity and wisdom of what was said, that you are just too stupid to 'get it', which is not a pleasant thought. Your confidence and self-esteem drop a point or two.

You console yourself with the knowledge that even though you still don't know what a 'maze' really is, at least you have something you can say if someone asks you about mazes: "When is a maze not a maze? ... when it's amazing!"

In a strange way you find those words are actually quite fascinating, comforting even. Even though they plainly don't make any sense at all, regardless of whether you know what a maze is, you feel that perhaps they really do hold a hidden gem of wisdom, and you'll see it if you think hard enough about it. But no matter how hard you think, the wisdom always remains just out of reach.

We could go on imagining your progress in the maze, but I suspect that by now you are either wondering what the point of it is, or perhaps you have already made an association between it and what it can be like for an inquisitive child to be born into a religious family. However, before we go any further, I want to emphasise that this book is neither about whether gods exist, nor what they want us to do (if they do exist). This book is about observable human behaviour.

The particular aspect of human behaviour given consideration in this book is how language is used to influence the thoughts and behaviour of other humans, and how particular styles of writing and word choice are used to do it. For illustration purposes I will use Mere Christianity by C. S. Lewis, a book lauded by many, and cited¹ by others as the book which led to their conversion to Christianity. It is for that reason - that it is an excellent example of influential writing - that I have chosen it as source material.

At the time I wrote this book, Mere Christianity could be read online at the Truth According To Scripture website² where it was also available as an audiobook or PDF download. In this book, wherever I cite page numbers it is to that PDF edition I refer. It is also widely available in print, or in ebook form. The Kindle version I have includes a Foreword by someone called Kathleen Norris, about whom I know nothing other than she wrote the Foreword, but otherwise the content is practically identical to the PDF, although as an ebook it does of course lack page numbers.

The choice of Greece as the location for the maze in the title of this book was not arbitrary. We can thank the Greek philosophers for giving us the tools to analyse what people say, or write, to see if it contains any errors of logic, or more simply, to see if it actually makes sense. But fear not, there is no requirement to read Greek philosophy to understand this book any more than it is a requirement to read religious scripture to understand Mere Christianity. Just as Lewis's book presents Christianity from the perspective of an 'ordinary man', this book adopts a similar perspective.

In his Preface, Lewis wrote:

" It is only a question of using words so that we can all understand what is being said.

In the next chapter we'll begin to take a look at how Lewis used words, and we'll use some of that Greek philosophy stuff to help us do it.

Reference Links for Chapter 1

1 Cultural impact: http://goo.gl/Qt9kAh
2 Mere Christianity online: http://goo.gl/Xwwjn

Chapter 2 • All Greek To Me

In the previous chapter I made reference to the Greek philosophers. To begin this chapter I will refer to just one; the one who was responsible for defining the basic analytical tools to which I alluded. By way of introduction, let me quote from the well respected scholar and historian, Brian G. Templeford, whose special interest in the life and times of the ancient Greeks has earned him many accolades, not least of which was the Lustran prize for History (2004). Templeford[1] describes our Greek philosopher thus:

> Born in 384 BCE, in the city of Stagira, the only son of Nichomacus and Amaltheia, it was not until late adolescence that Zakharias changed his given name to Aristotle, having observed that the conventions of the time tended to favour those whose names came first alphabetically. Not much is known about his childhood, but after studying under Plato (himself a student of Socrates), Aristotle went on to shape much of Western philosophy as we know it today, his writings encompassing ethics, aesthetics, logic, science, politics, astronomy, and metaphysics.

For our purposes we will concentrate on Aristotle's work on logic, and in particular his 'Thirteen Fallacies', but first it might be beneficial to define what a 'fallacy' actually is:

> A fallacy is a statement that is logically false, but one which often appears to be true.

That's simple enough, right? Unfortunately, it's not always simple to identify fallacies in 'real life'. Consider this sentence from page 15 of Mere Christianity:

> **"** If a man asked what was the point of playing football, it would not be much good saying "in order to score goals," for trying to score goals is the game itself, not the reason for the game, and you would really only be saying that football was football - which is true, but not worth saying.

Let's unravel that sentence, starting with the stated question "what is the point of playing football?". If we take it to mean "what is the objective?" - a reasonable interpretation given the many meanings of the word 'point' - then "to try to score goals" is a perfectly reasonable answer. The reason Lewis gave for that answer being "not much good" is that it is "not the reason for the game". But that only makes sense if the word 'point' in the question is taken to mean 'reason for' (further interpreted to mean 'underlying reason for' or 'reason behind'). And if we interpret the question in that way, then to answer "to try to score goals" is not just "not much good", it's absurd. It says nothing about competition, fun, exercise, winning, team spirit, all the things which form part of the 'reason for' the game. Blurring the differences in the meaning of the word 'point' makes the sentence sound 'deep' when it is actually meaningless.

There is something else in there which is worthy of note - the assertion that "trying to score goals is the game itself". What exactly is meant by "the game itself"? It's not clear what it means, and no explanation is given, but it is presented as a self-evident fact. Given what we have already noted about the sentence, the use of the phrase "the game itself" seems to be a means to avoid saying "the objective of the game", which would rather expose the fallacy in all its hidden glory. Lewis's phrasing has the hallmarks of a bit of literary magic dust thrown in to disguise the fallacy.

As for the conclusion that it "would really only be saying that football was football - which is true, but not worth saying", well at least saying "football is football" *is* true, which is more than can be said for the sentence in its entirety. Bearing in mind that Lewis inserted this sentence as an analogy to clarify the meaning of both the sentence before it and the one after, we could justifiably view it as the equivalent of scoring an own goal.

Effectively, what the unravelled sentence establishes is this: That there are two questions which could be asked about football. The first is "what is the objective when playing football?" and the second is "what is the underlying reason for the game of football?". To answer "to try to score goals" to both questions would demonstrate, at best, a lack of understanding of the difference between them, and at worst a wilful attempt to deceive.

It tends to be a lot harder unravelling fallacies than it is to write them (at least I find it so), but I think it is worth the effort, especially if you are the sort of person who is genuinely interested in getting to the bottom of things (sometimes called 'the truth'). If you are, then you might be wondering which of Aristotle's thirteen fallacies is at play in that sentence? The short answer is, "who cares?"

The slightly longer and more helpful answer is that if you want to learn about Aristotle's fallacies (and many more besides the thirteen identified by him) then you would do much better to make use of the internet, or failing that, visit a library, where you will find abundant literature on the subject. You could do worse than visiting the Changing Minds website[2].

The fallacy in Lewis's sentence is probably what Aristotle called Equivocation: using a word which has two or more different meanings. However, what I want to avoid is getting bogged down in nomenclature which, in the field of logical fallacies, can (rather ironically) get quite confusing. Common labels for fallacious arguments include Latin ones (eg. 'Ad Hominem'[3]), 'Appeals *to something*' (eg. Authority), 'Arguments *from something*' (eg. Ignorance), and 'False *somethings*' (eg. Dichotomy). For our purposes, it is not necessary to be able to instantly identify and correctly name any particular fallacy when we see it. We simply need to be able to detect when something we read or hear doesn't quite make sense, and work out why.

It's easy to fall into the trap of thinking it's our own fault if we struggle to make sense of something we read, to assume that we are not bright enough to understand the deep nuance of what is written. It may actually be true sometimes, but often enough it's a flag that the writer has indulged in a bit of fallacy-laden argument.

The use of fallacies in writing is sometimes accidental, by which I mean the writer is as much fooled by the fallacious arguments as the reader, and sometimes deliberate, where the writer knowingly tries to manipulate readers' thoughts. It's very easy to do, and to prove the point, here is one I prepared earlier...

If you are not familiar with Aristotle, then you probably accepted the information given in the paragraph about him at the beginning of this chapter (the paragraph in italics which I attributed to scholar and historian, Brian G Templeford). You might have accepted the information in that paragraph without my 'Appeal to Authority' (in the guise of good old Brian G), but it's a technique which is often used to add plausibility to a claim. The thing is, Brian G. Templeford is a figment of my imagination, as is the Lustran prize for History.

Sorry about that, especially if I've offended you, but what is perhaps worse is that I made up some of the information about Aristotle too. As far as I know, his father's name was indeed Nichomacus, but his mother's name was Phaestis, not Amaltheia, which is just a name I find rather attractive. Aristotle, not Zakharias, was his given name, which obviously means that I made up the part about him changing it. I also slipped 'astronomy' into the list of his writings. However, to the best of my knowledge, everything else is true.

Except he did have siblings (Arimneste and Arimnestus)[4]. But everything else is true. No, really. Honestly.

Of course the 'fallacy' in my paragraph about Aristotle has a very simple name. It's called lying. But the reason for all this subterfuge is to make the point that nothing should be taken as true just because it is in print, or simply because it is asserted. Assertions need to be backed up with evidence of their veracity, but the evidence itself needs checking for flaws. Sadly, sometimes evidence is rigged to look more genuine than it really is. Take, for example, the reference link I provided for Brian G. Templeford. If you didn't bother to check it, then you won't know that the referenced link actually takes you to a webpage which I happen to find rather amusing, and that it is not a reference to anything remotely Templefordian. Of course, if someone really wanted to pull the wool over your eyes, they could set a very plausible looking link to a non-existent page at Wikipedia, or another site, like this:

http://en.wikipedia.org/wiki/Brian_G_Templeford#Aristotle

We'll be exploring more fallacies in the ensuing chapters, but before we do, it's time to drag out another of those pesky Greek philosophers. This time, let me introduce to you, the one and only Eubulides (of Miletus), famous according to some sources, among philosophers at least, for having invented the 'liar paradox' (and six others) way back in the fourth century BCE, the same century in which Aristotle lived.

So one day Eubulides and Aristotle walked into a bar, and Eubulides said to the barman, "Aristotle always tells the truth."

Aristotle turned to the barman and said, "Eubulides always tells lies."

The barman turned to them both and said, "Yeah, very funny. Who's going to pay for the drinks?"

Eubulides and Aristotle both replied, in two-part harmony because they were that way inclined, "He is."[5]

And there you have a rather dodgy version of Eubulides's Liar Paradox, which can be stated much more simply in the single sentence, "I always tell lies". To be fair (although to whom I'm being fair is debatable - you, perhaps?), I should mention Epimenides, a philosopher and native of the island of Crete who is credited with saying, "Όλες οι Κρητικοί είναι ψεύτες". His big mistake was living two hundred or so years before Aristotle (which makes his inclusion in this book as Aristotle's drinking buddy a stretch too far), and also saying things in Greek, which sadly I don't understand. It's just as well there are translation services available which inform me that, in English, he said "All Cretans are liars". Quite why those sources mentioned above cite Eubulides rather than Epimenides as having invented the Liar Paradox is not clear to me. It's almost paradoxical.

You could spend eternity trying to solve the Liar Paradox, but we can quickly see it doesn't make sense to try, and there would be very little benefit to anyone if we did. Philosophers would probably disagree with that statement, and if you would like to know why, The Internet Encyclopedia of Philosophy webpage[6] about the Liar Paradox is probably as good a place to start as any. Oddly though, even for those of us who can sense the dangerous 'black hole' nature of paradoxes, they still seem to hold a fascination, tempting us to go back and make one more attempt to get our heads round them. Our overriding desire to understand and solve problems means we don't want to accept defeat, even though we know a solution is probably impossible.

That's fertile ground for anyone in the business of persuading others to this or that way of thinking (and often, buying). "Blue is the new black", "less is more". These are relatively modern instances of paradoxical statements being used as promotional slogans, and are examples of what I will call soft paradoxes. By 'soft' I mean they appear to hint at a hidden concept, an insight, or deeper meaning, despite not making sense when taken at face value. 'Hard' paradoxes are those such as "I always tell lies" which leave very little room, if any, for imaginative interpretation, their nature being that of academic puzzles. Both types appear in Mere Christianity:

" We are thinking about something that happened before Nature was created at all, *before time began*. (p71)

The italics are mine, and it is those three italicised words which are an example of a hard paradox. After all, the word 'before' depends on the existence of time for it to mean anything (because it is a description of a section in the continuum of time). Without time, there can be no before. Lewis just left it there, hanging on the end of his sentence, as if it answered a question rather than posed one, so it's unclear whether he knew he'd used the shifting sands of a paradox to support his argument.

A rather good example of the soft variety occurs on page 99:

> **❝** Your real, new self (which is Christ's and also yours, and yours just because it is His) ...

Wut!?

That sort of soft paradox is often used to inject an element of mystery which, to some, suggests profundity. Mystification (that is the act of injecting mystery - more bluntly described as the use of language to obfuscate meaning) occupies the opposite end of the scale on which 'clarification' can be found.

In the next chapter, we'll take a look at some more techniques used to persuade others to a particular way of thinking or point of view. But before we leave this chapter, here's one more soft paradox, also from page 99, for your delectation.

> **❝** The more we get what we now call "ourselves" out of the way and let Him take us over, the more truly ourselves we become.

Notes and Reference Links for Chapter 2

1 BGT: http://goo.gl/S6bbvj

2 Changing Minds: http://goo.gl/EZhg7t

3 Ad hominem definition: http://goo.gl/YgjQqa

4 Siblings: http://goo.gl/k7gnBR

5 Eubulides was a very generous chap, or possibly just tired from all the thinking he'd been doing. Or was it Aristotle?

6 IEP: http://www.iep.utm.edu/par-liar/

Chapter 3 • Hey Baldy!
Everybody Knows It's True!

If you spent your 'learning years' in an English speaking country then when you read the word 'God' (with a capital 'G'), I suspect you will think of the god of Christianity, regardless of whether or not you know that his 'real' name was Yahwey (or YHWH, or Jehovah). In everyday language, 'God' is used as his name or title. It is similar to how the word 'Führer' with a capital 'F' is automatically associated with Adolf Hitler, even though the actual meaning of the word 'führer' is simply 'leader' or 'guide'. There is also a convention that any third person reference to God-with-a-capital-G, or any of his constituent parts, requires the capitalisation of the 'H' in the words 'he', 'him', and 'his'.

Bearing this in mind, consider what Lewis wrote on page 19:

❝ And we have not yet got as far as a personal God - only as far as a power, ...

It's an example of a bold claim which is not supported by the facts. What makes it bold, audacious even, is that in the two pages immediately prior to that sentence, Lewis used the 'capitalised' word 'He' (as a reference to the 'power') six times. If it was "only a power", why didn't Lewis use 'it' rather than 'He' when referring to it? Lewis audaciously claimed that he hadn't got as far as a 'personal God' while consistently referring to that not-a-personal-god using the word 'He' (a *personal* pronoun). I haven't a clue if saying one thing while at the same time actually doing the opposite is 'officially' recognised as a fallacy, and I don't feel like researching it, so I will call it the Argument from Audacity.

Audacious or not, the sentence which immediately precedes the one we've just looked at is this:

" Only a Person can forgive.

Hold on a doggone minute thar pardner! Who says only a person with a capital P can forgive? Does a person need a capital P in order to exercise the attribute of forgiveness, or can any old person exercise it? Perhaps they need to be bald as well? In any event, it is without doubt a bald assertion.

The 'Bald Assertion' is an 'officially' recognised fallacy (if the fact that an internet search will find several instances of it being named and explained can qualify it as 'official'). It's very simple to do. Just make a statement, out of the blue, with nothing to back it up, as if it is self-evidently true.

"Blue-eyed people are better than those with brown eyes. They empathise with the plight of brown-eyed people much more than brown-eyed people empathise with the plight of blue-eyed people, and that's why blue-eyed people are better people."

Nothing wrong with that, right? Everybody knows that blue-eyed people are best'. And there we have Bald Assertion's close friend and associate, the Argument from Everybody Knows. I found three and a half examples of the Argument from Everybody Knows in Mere Christianity. The 'half' is because in the example on page 61 he wrote...

" I think everyone knows what I mean.

...which, because of the "I think", is only balding rather

18

than fully bald.

If you are checking up on my allegations, the other three examples can be found on pages 10 (in the guise of "We all know"), 46 and 93. And in case you haven't worked out what's wrong with it, I'd just like to point out that everybody knows that Everybody Knows is a fallacious argument, all except you apparently, which makes you a minuscule minority whose opinion, if you even have one, is totally worthless because absolutely nobody agrees with you.

'Everybody Knows' has what looks like a poor cousin; the Argument From Most People. It goes like this (the italics are mine):

" ... though there are differences between the moral ideas of one time or country and those of another, the differences are not really very great - not nearly so great as *most people* imagine - and you can recognise the same law running through them all ... (p12)

" But, of course, when they ask for a lead from the Church *most people* mean they want the clergy to put out a political programme. (p40)

" *Most* of the bored, discontented, rich *people* in the world are of this type. (p62)

There's a twist in the Argument from Most People though which makes it different from the Argument from Everybody Knows, and it's this: The Argument from Most People is often used to suggest that the minority camp is actually the place you really ought to be.

I know you probably know the word 'know' is a loathsome beast, and a known cloak of weasels, but I know you will agree that knowledge of its many guises will put you in the know, and therefore, you will knowingly want to know more. Yeah, right. What do I know?

I'm glad you asked because the word 'know' so often gets used to give extra weight to an assertion. 'Knowing' something implies there is no doubt about it, that it is a fact, an unassailable truth. No one (except me, possibly, but I'll come to that later) would dispute that two plus two equals four, and it is sometimes used to demonstrate what it means to know something as a fact or universal truth. Lewis used it in a round about kind of way on page 9:

" You might just as well try to imagine a country where two and two made five.

Some claimants, when confronted with the fact that some knowledge claims can be backed up with a mountain of evidence, while others, such as theirs, have very little or no evidence to support them, have alluded to different 'ways of knowing'. Well that's handy. Maybe I can make use of that.

"Only a Person can forgive". Remember Lewis's assertion? Well, I dispute it. My dogs (I have four of them at the moment) forgive me quite regularly. Willie in particular, who is a bit excitable, tends to forget the rules in his excitement which sometimes leads to a smack on the snout to remind him. He forgives me for reminding him within a very short time, mere seconds. In fact I think he would forgive me anything.

Now I could use one of Lewis's techniques here, and have a conversation with an imaginary person[2] in order to prove my point, but that would be using what I will call the Argument from He Said She Said, which I'll expand on later. Let's just pretend I've had the conversation and I've finished up with, "everybody knows that dogs are the most forgiving of animals."

Unfortunately for me, my imaginary friend and interlocutor is a bit uppity and won't just meekly accept my Argument from Everybody Knows, retorting with, "How do you know that your dog's behaviour is real forgiveness? If he is not aware that he is forgiving you then it is not real forgiveness."

Rather than actually answer her question, or even tackle her Bald Assertion, I say there are more ways than one of knowing something, finishing with, "I know it in my heart that my dogs not only forgive me, but love me too."

It doesn't really matter how my uppity friend responds because she is just an imaginary person, so we'll let her wander off into an imaginary sunset, and have her singing, "Keep them dogies[3] rollin' Rawhide!" as she goes, just because we can.

Meanwhile, back at the ranch, we are left to delve into this idea of different ways of knowing. Do I really know it in my heart that my dogs not only forgive me, but love me too? Well, of course not! My heart is a muscular organ which pumps blood around my body. Nothing more, nothing less[4]. What is meant by that expression is that even though I can't necessarily prove it as a 'scientific fact', I am fully convinced of it, not only because I have the evidence of my personal experience with my dogs, but because my emotional self feels it to be true.

So now we have to ask ourselves, "Is that a valid way of knowing something?"

I'm hopeful that we agree the answer is, "It depends on what the *something* is."

For example, it's probably obvious that someone who says that eating a kilogram of green banana skins on a Tuesday will keep us free of cancer because they *know it in their heart* is not to be trusted. I don't actually know if eating any amount of banana skins (of any colour, on any day of the week) is harmful, but it seems likely there would be no benefits, and quite possibly some harm. For those sorts of claims we quite rightly demand more rigorous evidence because accepting it on the basis that someone knows it in their heart could have undesirable consequences.

So it seems the consequences of accepting a knowledge claim can play a sizeable part in our attitude to 'ways of knowing'. The more serious the possible consequences of accepting a piece of information, the more rigorously we pay attention to the 'way of knowing' employed to assert it. This results in the unfortunate, and sometimes despicable, tendency to try to 'upgrade' a knowledge claim by disguising it as one that has come about via a 'way of knowing' which is more rigorous than the one actually employed.

I said earlier that I might dispute that two plus two equals four, and now seems an appropriate time to explain why, and why it matters. I'm not daft enough to claim that $2 + 2 = 5$, but I can state absolutely categorically that $2 + 2 = 11$. And what's more I can prove it.

There is nothing magical about it, it adheres to the rules of mathematics just as much as $2 + 2 = 4$ does. All that is necessary is to define the system of numbers we are using to be ternary[5] rather than decimal (the number system we happen to use as the default, which is to say it is a convention). In ternary there are only three recognised numbers: 0, 1 and 2 (similar to the more

22

widely known binary system which only uses 0 and 1).

In binary, 2 + 2 is meaningless because the symbol we call 'two' is not recognised as a number. But in ternary, 2 + 2 is recognised and computes to 11 (which I think purists would say as "one one" rather than "eleven"). The ternary sequence of numbers (with the decimal equivalents below) begins like this:

0	1	2	10	**11**	12	20	21	22	100	101	...
0	1	2	3	**4**	5	6	7	8	9	10	...

Yeah. Okay. Very clever. So what?

Mathematics is sometimes portrayed as an ultimate truth, a standard against which other purported truths can be compared. Lewis made reference to mathematics in his attempt to prove the existence of the 'Law of Human Nature', describing mathematics, on page 12, as a 'real truth'. He put his case like this:

❝ We all learned the multiplication table at school. A child who grew up alone on a desert island would not know it. But surely it does not follow that the multiplication table is simply a human convention, something human beings have made up for themselves and might have made different if they had liked? I fully agree that we learn the Rule of Decent Behaviour from parents and teachers, and friends and books, as we learn everything else. But some of the things we learn are mere conventions which might have been different - we learn to keep to the left of the road, but it might just as well have been the rule to keep to the right - and others of them, like mathematics, are real truths.

Well, seeing as you asked, my dear departed Lewis,

humans could indeed have made the multiplication table different if they had so chosen, for example by adopting ternary rather than decimal as the convention, which rather kicks the legs out from under the argument.

Mathematics lends itself to the sort of reasoning Lewis employed because firstly it is universally agreed that 2 + 2 (decimal) = 4 regardless of nationality, politics, or world view, and secondly because it is something which can be said to be 'outside' of human existence, in as much as two plus two (decimal) would still equal four even if there were no humans alive to know it. However, while that might technically be true, without humans, or some other creatures intelligent enough to understand and make use of it, mathematics is redundant. Nothing more than the sound of one hand clapping. Lewis made reference to mathematics at several other points in his book, but I'll leave it to you to check out if he used one or two hands on those occasions. The relevant pages are 29, 32, 38, & 53.

In the next chapter, we'll get sexy.

Notes and Reference Links for Chapter 3

1 You might know that I borrowed the blue-eyed versus brown-eyed idea from Jane Elliott, but if you haven't seen it, the video might still be accessible here:

   http://goo.gl/DNWxCF

   Her website is here: http://www.janeelliott.com/

2 Here's a somewhat amusing example from page 25:

   I know someone will ask me, "Do you really mean, at this time of day, to reintroduce our old friend the devil - hoofs and horns and all?" Well, what the time of day has to do with it I do not know. And I am not particular about the hoofs and horns. But in other respects my answer is "Yes, I do."

3 Dogies versus doggies: http://goo.gl/pyhFpu

4 Heart 'neurons': http://goo.gl/yRCuZU

5 Ternary numbers: http://goo.gl/2Kf6L

Chapter 4 • Too Sexy For My Horsehair Shirt

Lewis didn't shrink in the face of sex, but rather took a full frontal approach, giving it one, whole section to itself, entitled 'Sexual Morality'. Ooh er missus! Well, that's got the innuendos out of the way so now we can get down to the business in hand.

On page 47 Lewis wrote:

> There are people who want to keep our sex instinct inflamed in order to make money out of us. Because, of course, a man with an obsession is a man who has very little sales-resistance.

It's recognisable as a more convoluted way of saying 'sex sells'. More interesting for now, though, is the technique Lewis used to persuade his readers that our sexual instinct has 'gone wrong' which, he claimed, has resulted in an abundance of 'unchastity'. Unchastity, according to Lewis, is anything which does not fall within the bounds of 'chastity', about which he said:

> ... the old Christian rule is, "Either marriage, with complete faithfulness to your partner, or else total abstinence." (p45)

There is sufficient evidence in Mere Christianity to support the view that Lewis was a lover of analogies. In his foray into sexual morality, he presented the sexual instinct as analogous to the instinct to eat, and, also on page 45, he set the analogy up like this:

> The biological purpose of sex is children, just as the biological purpose of eating is to repair the body.

'Repair' is probably not the word I would have chosen, 'sustain' or 'nourish' seeming better choices, but let's not quibble. Let's see where he went with it:

> ❝ Now if we eat whenever we feel inclined and just as much as we want, it is quite true that most of us will eat too much: but not terrifically too much. One man may eat enough for two, but he does not eat enough for ten. The appetite goes a little beyond its biological purpose, but not enormously. But if a healthy young man indulged his sexual appetite whenever he felt inclined, and if each act produced a baby, then in ten years he might easily populate a small village. This appetite is in ludicrous and preposterous excess of its function.

He extended the food analogy in a second paragraph.

> ❝ You can get a large audience together for a strip-tease act - that is, to watch a girl undress on the stage. Now suppose you came to a country where you could fill a theatre by simply bringing a covered plate on to the stage and then slowly lifting the cover so as to let every one see, just before the lights went out, that it contained a mutton chop or a bit of bacon, would you not think that in that country something had gone wrong with the appetite for food? And would not anyone who had grown up in a different world think there was something equally queer about the state of the sex instinct among us?

I'm going to call what's going on in those two paragraphs The Argument from Trees, because Lewis apparently could not see the wood (forest, or bush) for the trees.

In the first paragraph, Lewis attempted to show that our sexual instinct has 'gone wrong' by comparing it to our instinct to consume food. We'll ignore his Argument from Most Of Us in the first sentence, and home in on the second:

>❝ One man may eat enough for two, but he does not eat enough for ten.

The use of the words "does not" is ambiguous, because it allows an interpretation that the man makes a choice, but if the man is truly indulging his appetite without restriction then he simply comes to a point where he *cannot* eat any more. It's not a matter of choice to stop after eating enough for two, it's a physical impossibility to continue. We could argue over whether the man Lewis spoke of was capable of eating enough for two or three, or any other number, but the point is he would reach his capacity, and that would be the deciding factor regarding how much he ate. His instinct is to eat to capacity[1] which is no different to his instinct to indulge his sexual appetite to capacity. In each case there may be other factors, for example availability, or peer pressure, which will influence how close to capacity he gets, but at root, both instincts drive him there.

The second paragraph also employs the food analogy. In that paragraph, the wood in which The Argument from Trees resides is called a restaurant.

A restaurant? Let me explain. In restaurants the world over, food dishes are brought to tables with the food arranged in fancy ways to titillate the senses of patrons. The platters are not necessarily covered, but it is often the case that until they reach the table, the temptations they hold are not clearly visible, teasing the desires of

29

their intended recipients, who, it should be remembered, are paying for their seats in this 'theatre of food'. Perhaps the dish which best illustrates the similarity between Lewis's strip-tease act and restaurant food is the roast joint which arrives at table hidden by a domed silver cover which is not removed until the table is fully laden. Now if Lewis's assertion that "the biological purpose of eating is to repair the body" is correct, then using Lewisian criteria, all this playing around with food can reasonably be taken as evidence that something has 'gone wrong' with our appetite for food, perhaps even more so than Lewis claimed of our sexual appetite.

But Lewis apparently couldn't see it. In a subsequent paragraph he wrote:

" You find very few people who want to eat things that really are not food or to do other things with food instead of eating it. In other words, perversions of the food appetite are rare.

Chewing gum? Or is that not classed as eating? Cooking? Or is cooking not "doing other things with food instead of eating it"? If you think about it you can see that the actual eating is a very small part of what we do with food. Much of what we do with food, the preparation, cooking and presentation of it, merely panders to our 'perverted' appetites. Think of the phrase sometimes used about an 'exotic' food: *It's an acquired taste.* Perversion, it seems, just as much as beauty, is in the eye of the beholder. Check it out next time you eat in a restaurant, and see if you can see the wood Lewis apparently missed.

But wait, we're not yet done with The Argument from Trees. I wrote at the beginning of this chapter that Lewis had presented a version of 'sex sells', and the second sentence from the quote is pertinent:

❝ Because, of course, a man with an obsession is a man who has very little sales-resistance.

I won't argue with that because I think it's generally true. But throughout his book Lewis presents the world as if it's principal and most important inhabitants are men. In his chapter on Sexual Morality, it doesn't seem to occur to him that men are not the only ones to have a sexual appetite. He spoke of the sexual instinct as having 'gone wrong', but the argument he presented only addressed the male half of the population, and completely ignored the sexual instincts of women (most shamefully in his wild scenario relying on vast numbers of anonymous women to accommodate his "healthy young man").

But it's not just his dealings with sexual issues in which women were almost invisible. In the entire book he used the words 'man' or 'men' 395 times, 'human' or 'humans' 121 times, but 'woman' or 'women' only 25 times. It rather suggests that the book itself is an Argument from Trees, where women are the forest.

Lewis consistently referred specifically to 'a man' where it would have been a simple matter to make a reference to 'someone'. Some examples:

❝ You would not call **a man** humane for ceasing to set mousetraps ... (p13)

❝ If **a man** asked what was the point of playing football ... (p15)

❝ We call a cancer bad, they would say, because it kills **a man** ... (p21)

31

«« God made us: invented us as **a man** invents an engine. (p27)

«« When **a man** makes a moral choice two things are involved. (p42)

«« Greed will certainly make **a man** want money ... (p56)

«« If **a man** has "charity," ... (p59)

«« But supposing **a man's** reason ... (p63)

«« When **a man** has made these two discoveries ... (p65)

But don't get too smug and complacent if you are a man who sees nothing wrong with Lewis's male-centric view. Just being male isn't enough:

«« God can show Himself as He really is only to real men. (p74)

And there you have it. An unadulterated and blatant Appeal to Real Men[tm].

I'll go into the Appeal to Real Men[tm] in the next chapter, but there is more to be said about Lewis's attitude to women and the role they should take in society. Perhaps the most illustrative example is on pages 52 and 53, where Lewis wrote about Christian marriage. He began by stating facts and then asked two questions about them:

«« Christian wives promise to obey their husbands. In Christian marriage the man is said to be the "head". Two questions obviously arise here, (1) Why should there be a head at all - why not equality? (2) Why should it be the man?

Lewis went on to provide answers to his questions. We'll take a look at his answer to question 1 first:

> **"** (1) The need for some head follows from the idea that marriage is permanent. Of course, as long as the husband and wife are agreed, no question of a head need arise; and we may hope that this will be the normal state of affairs in a Christian marriage. But when there is a real disagreement, what is to happen? Talk it over, of course; but I am assuming they have done that and still failed to reach agreement What do they do next? They cannot decide by a majority vote, for in a council of two there can be no majority. Surely, only one or other of two things can happen: either they must separate and go their own ways or else one or other of them must have a casting vote. If marriage is permanent, one or other party must, in the last resort, have the power of deciding the family policy. You cannot have a permanent association without a constitution.

Firstly, he didn't explain why or how the need for some head *follows* from the idea that marriage is permanent, although he made another Bald Assertion in the final sentence of the paragraph that "you cannot have a permanent association without a constitution". This, however, does not demonstrate the need for a 'head', even if he was correct about the 'constitution'.

Secondly, having established that even in a Christian marriage there will be times when a couple will fail to agree, and that there can be no majority vote with only two people, he came to the conclusion that either they must separate or one of them must have a casting vote; that in a permanent marriage one or other party must have the deciding vote. What Lewis appeared to think but failed to prove is that it always has to be the *same party* who has the deciding vote. Nevertheless, Lewis moved on to provide an answer to his second question (Why should it be the man?):

66 (2) If there must be a head, why the man? Well, firstly, is there any very serious wish that it should be the woman? As I have said, I am not married myself, but as far as I can see, even a woman who wants to be the head of her own house does not usually admire the same state of things when she finds it going on next door. She is much more likely to say "Poor Mr. X! Why he allows that appalling woman to boss him about the way she does is more than I can imagine." I do not think she is even very flattered if anyone mentions the fact of her own "headship." There must be something unnatural about the rule of wives over husbands, because the wives themselves are half ashamed of it and despise the husbands whom they rule. But there is also another reason; and here I speak quite frankly as a bachelor, because it is a reason you can see from outside even better than from inside. The relations of the family to the outer world - what might be called its foreign policy - must depend, in the last resort, upon the man, because he always ought to be, and usually is, much more just to the outsiders. A woman is primarily fighting for her own children and husband against the rest of the world. Naturally, almost, in a sense, rightly, their claims override, for her, all other claims. She is the special trustee of their interests. The function of the husband is to see that this natural preference of hers is not given its head. He has the last word in order to protect other people from the intense family patriotism of the wife. If anyone doubts this, let me ask a simple question. If your dog has bitten the child next

door, or if your child has hurt the dog next door, which would you sooner have to deal with, the master of that house or the mistress? Or, if you are a married woman, let me ask you this question. Much as you admire your husband, would you not say that his chief failing is his tendency not to stick up for his rights and yours against the neighbours as vigorously as you would like? A bit of an Appeaser?

Bearing in mind that Lewis failed to establish that there needs to be a single permanent 'head' who always has the casting vote, perhaps it's not surprising that his attempt to show why it should be the man started out by pooh-poohing the very notion that anyone would think otherwise. By dismissing an idea as trivial - laughable even - it can make the job of arguing against it a lot easier. Let's call it the Argument from Trivialisation.

Because the rest of the paragraph is based on the flawed premise that there needs to be a single permanent 'head' who always has the casting vote, his illustrations and the conclusions he drew are equally flawed. Perhaps the most telling sentence is this one:

❝ The relations of the family to the outer world - what might be called its foreign policy - must depend, in the last resort, upon the man, because he always ought to be, and usually is, much more just to the outsiders.

Why *ought* a man be more just to outsiders than a woman? Lewis didn't say, but made the Bald Assertion that they usually are, and padded it with general anecdotes about women's alleged motivations and behaviour. But surely *everyone* ought to strive to be just to outsiders, regardless of gender? The Argument from Ought is lazy at best, and pernicious at worst.

I have no evidence to back it up, apart from what Lewis wrote in the paragraphs quoted above, and others, but I suspect that Lewis was not, or would not have been, a fan of Robert Ingersoll, who said in his 1887 lecture *The Liberty of Man, Woman and Child*[2]:

> **❝** If there is any man I detest, it is the man who thinks he is the head of a family – the man who thinks he is 'boss!'...
>
> Imagine a young man and a young woman courting, walking out in the moonlight, and the nightingale singing a song of pain and love, as though the thorn touched her heart – imagine them stopping there in the moonlight and starlight and song, and saying, "Now, here, let us settle who is boss!" I tell you it is an infamous word and an infamous feeling – I abhor a man who is 'boss', who is going to govern in his family, and when he speaks orders all the rest to be still as some mighty idea is about to be launched from his mouth. Do you know I dislike this man unspeakably?

While we are on the topic of the sexes, here are a couple of examples of what I will call the Argument from Disparaging Women, a tactic which may well appeal to the Real Men[tm] who Lewis was apparently targeting:

> **❝** What makes a pretty girl spread misery wherever she goes by collecting admirers? Certainly not her sexual instinct: that kind of girl is quite often sexually frigid. (p57)

> **❝** We must get over wanting to be needed: in some goodish people, specially women, that is the hardest of all temptations to resist. (p98)

Before I close this chapter, in case you are wondering about alternatives to having a single permanent 'head' who always has the casting vote, one alternative is this. Both parties agree that the deciding vote for issues upon which they can find no compromise will alternate between them. On this occasion the deciding vote will be with one party, on the next it will be with the other. Of course, who gets the first deciding vote could be an issue, but that is what a flip of a coin can decide.

Notes and Reference Links for Chapter 4

1 Although it may not have been as obvious in the middle of the last century (at the time Lewis wrote), the large number of obese people is ample evidence that people eat to capacity.

2 Robert Ingersoll: http://goo.gl/LKm9Tk

Chapter 5 • Pink Or Blue?

So you are either one of those people who reads random chapters, or you decided to continue reading from the previous chapter to see what I would say about the Appeal to Real Men™. Am I right, or am I right?

Whatever your reason for being here, I think the Appeal to Real Men™ is fairly obvious, but just to be sure: it's the suggestion that as a man you are at best weak, timid, easily led, lacklustre, insignificant, possibly effeminate, and definitely not worthy of respect unless you agree with, adopt, and promote whatever it is the person making the appeal is promoting (who is, of course, a Real Man™), and thereby establish your credentials as a Real Man™ as well.

Now it goes without saying that you are either happy with that definition or you are not, but there seems little I can do about it, so if you don't like it you will just have to lump it. And if any of that makes you feel uncomfortable, then it might well be because I attempted to force you into one or other of only two positions when there are other positions which you might reasonably hold. I'll call it the Argument from Either Or, an example of which is embodied in the first paragraph of this chapter.

I've called it the Argument from Either Or because that seems to be the most common form of it, a choice between two things, but it also applies where any limited number of choices are presented which exclude valid alternatives. Also known as a False Dichotomy, Lewis employed the Argument from Either Or several times in Mere Christianity. Page 28 is a rich source:

❝ A man who was merely a man and said the sort of things Jesus said would not be a great moral teacher. He would either be a lunatic - on a level with the man who says he is a poached egg - or else he would be the Devil of Hell.

❝ Either this man was, and is, the Son of God: or else a madman or something worse.

❝ We are faced, then, with a frightening alternative. This man we are talking about either was (and is) just what He said or else a lunatic, or something worse.

The first example is a true Argument from Either Or. Ignoring whether the bald assertion in the first sentence is true, the two options given exclude other possibilities. The man could have rational reasons for genuinely believing what he said was for the benefit of humankind, he could be a figment of someone else's imagination (a legend), or he could just be a bit naughty, a comedian perhaps. The second and third examples offer three alternatives (God, lunatic, or 'something worse'), but once again there are other possibilities just as in the first example.

Page 43 contains another striking example:

❝ ... the real, free choice of the man, on the material presented to him, either to put his own advantage first or to put it last.

Plainly there are many more options than just two. 'First' and 'last' mark the opposite ends of a scale on which there are an almost unlimited number of intermediate points.

The Argument from Either Or was quite a favourite

with Lewis. Here's one more example from page 86:

> 	In the end, you will either give up trying to be good, or
> 	else become one of those people who, as they say, "live
> 	for others" but always in a discontented, grumbling
> 	way - always wondering why the others do not notice
> 	it more and always making a martyr of yourself.

It's one of the easier fallacies to spot, so I'll leave it to
you, dear reader, to find other examples. However, let's
think a bit more about the Appeal to Real Men[tm]. It is in
effect an Argument from Either Or too. Either you are a
Real Man[tm] (good), or you are something else (bad). This
form of the argument is sometimes characterised as 'in
group, out group', or 'us and them', a blunt example
being the expression, "you're either with us, or agin us!"
(Said in your best 'rebel rousing' voice).

Promoting an 'in group, out group', 'us and them'
outlook is sometimes called 'othering'. It's purpose is to
draw people into the 'in group' ('us') by denigrating
people who are defined to be in the 'out group' ('them'),
which is achieved by defining 'them' as a group of
'others' who are somehow less valuable, or have no value
at all. It also serves to retain members of the 'in group'
within the fold. Mere Christianity could reasonably be
described as one giant exercise in othering, and the key
evidence for that assertion is Lewis's claim about the
Christian god revealing himself as he really is only to real
men. The full paragraph in which the claim is made, on
page 74, is as follows:

> 	God can show Himself as He really is only to real men.
> 	And that means not simply to men who are
> 	individually good, but to men who are united together

in a body, loving one another, helping one another, showing Him to one another. For that is what God meant humanity to be like; like players in one band, or organs in one body.

The inescapable implication of that paragraph is that humanity comprises only a sub-section of men, *real men*, as defined therein. Real Humanity™ perhaps? All other humans (women, children, and men who fall short of the criteria for real men) are well and truly 'othered' by their exclusion from 'humanity'. It probably should come as no surprise then that the only persons listed at Wikipedia as examples of people who converted to Christianity as a result of reading Mere Christianity are men: Charles Colson, Francis Collins, Jonathan Aitken, Josh Caterer and C. E. M. Joad.

This othering might seem as if it would be counter-productive; excluding - alienating even - large numbers of people who might otherwise join your group. There are two strategies to lessen the effect. The first is to make the in-group attractive to as many powerful, influential and privileged people as possible, by any means at your disposal. This can include both 'positive' methods (for example by flattery - suggesting that your special qualities make you especially eligible to be part of the in-group) and 'negative' (for example by the implication that no powerful, influential people of any worth are in the out-group). The second is to attempt to get as many people in the out-group to believe that the out-group is exactly where they should be, and that they should proudly support the in-group from there.

The second strategy is plainly more difficult than the first, and consequently a more indirect approach is often adopted. Take, for example, the paragraph we looked at in the previous chapter where Lewis was justifying why the man should be 'head'. These are the pertinent parts:

" ... even a woman who wants to be the head of her own house does not usually admire the same state of things when she finds it going on next door. She is much more likely to say "Poor Mr. X! Why he allows that appalling woman to boss him about the way she does is more than I can imagine." I do not think she is even very flattered if anyone mentions the fact of her own "headship."

" There must be something unnatural about the rule of wives over husbands, because the wives themselves are half ashamed of it and despise the husbands whom they rule.

" A woman is primarily fighting for her own children and husband against the rest of the world. Naturally, almost, in a sense, rightly, their claims override, for her, all other claims. She is the special trustee of their interests.

Reading through Mere Christianity, Lewis seemed hellbent on becoming the King of the Bald Assertion. On what did he base his assertion that "a woman who wants to be the head of her own house _does not usually_ admire the same state of things when she finds it going on next door"? How did he know that she "is _much more likely_ to say Poor Mr. X"? It was "as far as he could see", which may or may not have been very far. But putting the Bald Assertions to one side, he was presenting a model of how women think and behave (which just happened to match _his_ view of how they should think and behave) as if it is quite natural and normal for them to behave that way.

And cringeworthy though it is, he used the Argument from Faux Appreciation in regard to their 'special status' (in the form of "She is the special trustee of their interests") to imply that women are exceptionally important (but still, it went without saying, in a subordinate role to men).

There is something else about 'othering'. While it might seem a strange tactic to you or me because we think that inclusivity is the way forward, some groups could not function without an out-group who can be blamed for the failings of the in-group's teachings, policies, or doctrines. How can I claim to be one of the good guys if there are no bad guys 'out there'? Identifying the bad guys is an important part of the othering process. How odd it is that the 'bad *guys*' so often turn out to be the women.

Why is it, though, that some women appear to happily accept their subordinate position in the out-group and, what is more, defend it? I don't have a definitive answer to that, and I doubt there is one at present, but I'll make a wild conjecture that they fear that without the rules and expectations of the in-group to keep them in check, men would behave even more badly towards them.

Pink or Blue? I chose those colours because they are stereotypically associated with gender, something which has been a feature of this chapter. But let's not allow our growth to be stunted by stereotypes. Let's go green.

Chapter 6 • How Green Was My Valet?

Those of you who are aware of the novel by Richard Llewellyn[1] and/or the subsequent film directed by John Ford might like to take a moment to cringe or groan at that title, but regardless of how funny you think my attempts at amusing wordplay are, a straightforward answer to the question might be, "Why don't you ask him?"

It would certainly be better to ask him rather than assume your idea of his green-ness was a true representation of the reality. Or, if he is not available, then at the very least it would be wise to consult others who know or knew him. Lewis apparently understood that principle because in his Preface he took some pains to emphasise that he was presenting only what was common to all strains of Christianity rather than any particular version, and that he'd taken special care to avoid letting his own personal bias influence what he wrote:

" The danger clearly was that I should put forward as common Christianity anything that was peculiar to the Church of England _or (worse still) to myself_. I tried to guard against this by sending the original script of what is now Book Two to four clergymen (Anglican, Methodist, Presbyterian, Roman Catholic) and asking for their criticism. (p5 - emphasis is mine)

Further into the book, on pages 22 - 23, which form part of Book Two, he gave a brief explanation of how he came to accept Christianity (again the emphasis is mine):

" _My argument_ against God was that the universe seemed so cruel and unjust. But how had I got this idea of just and unjust? A man does not call a line crooked unless he has some idea of a straight line. What was I comparing this universe with when I called it unjust? If the whole show was bad and senseless from A to Z, so to speak, why did I, who was supposed to be part of the show, find myself in such violent reaction against it? A man feels wet when he falls into water, because man is not a water animal: a fish would not feel wet.

Of course I could have given up my idea of justice by saying it was nothing but a private idea of my own. But if I did that, then _my argument_ against God collapsed too - for the argument depended on saying that the world was really unjust, not simply that it did not happen to please my private fancies. Thus in the very act of trying to prove that God did not exist - in other words, that the whole of reality was senseless - I found I was forced to assume that one part of reality - namely my idea of justice - was full of sense.

Consequently atheism turns out to be too simple. If the whole universe has no meaning, we should never have found out that it has no meaning: just as, if there were no light in the universe and therefore no creatures with eyes, we should never know it was dark. Dark would be without meaning.

Very well then, atheism is too simple.

What Lewis did there is the very thing he thought so important to guard against in regard to how he presented Christianity. He described his _personal_ "argument against God", and how it fell apart, as if his personal argument equated to common atheism, or to borrow his terminology, 'mere atheism'. But atheism doesn't have an "argument against God" because atheism

46

holds that there are no gods, not even one, against whom an argument could be had.

His statement that the universe "seemed so cruel and unjust" is revealing. It implies that he already thought of the universe as some sort of entity capable of cruelty and judgement, which is not a 'common' position held by atheists. If he had applied the same standard that he used for his presentation of Christianity (by sending his script to four atheists asking for their criticism? I'm sure Bertrand Russell[2], for one, would have obliged) perhaps he would not have mistaken his view of the universe for atheism. That, of course, we will never know, but at least we have a good example of what I will call the Argument from Double Standards.

On the subject of 'green-ness', you might be thinking, "Is he really that green that he thinks, in all honesty, that he has been truly presenting 'fallacies' in Lewis's writing? He clearly doesn't know the first thing about fallacies and simply has something against Lewis, picking holes in his writing merely for the sake of it! Who does he think he is anyway?"

And if you really were thinking that, then apart from having an uncanny ability to phrase your thoughts in the style of Lewis, you have also asked questions, and questions deserve a response. And here it is: "No. Untrue. Me. In that order."

Not quite as fancy an answer as Lewis might have given, and if I had applied 'WWLS' (What Would Lewis Say) then I might have replied, "Well, quite what who I think I am has got to do with it I don't know, and my personal opinion of Lewis is neither here nor there - he seems a nice enough chap - but nevertheless, I stand by what I have presented as 'fallacious' in his writing in as much as they are examples of faulty reasoning or practice."

Thinking about those two rather contrasting styles of answer, the first response is definitely blunt, probably verging on contemptuous, and offers little to commend it as an aid to understanding. On the other hand, the WWLS version, although perhaps coming across as condescending, does at least put some meat on the bones (and also manages to make me - the responder - seem like a 'nice chap' via the "nice enough chap" reference to Lewis). Of course the style in which a question is posed has a role in how we feel about the response, and if we compose both the question and the answer then we control all aspects of the 'exchange'.

In Chapter 3 I mentioned the Argument from He Said She Said. However, it's got nothing to do with gender, it's about creating an imaginary conversation, or exchange, in order to 'prove a point'. Here's an example from page 15:

" If we ask: "Why ought I to be unselfish?" and you reply "Because it is good for society," we may then ask, "Why should I care what's good for society except when it happens to pay me personally?" and then you will have to say, "Because you ought to be unselfish" - which simply brings us back to where we started. You are saying what is true, but you are not getting any further.

That comes immediately before Lewis's scoring-goals-in-football analogy which we looked at in Chapter 2. But of course the conversation could have gone differently...

You: Why ought I to be unselfish?
Me: Because I'll smack you in the mouth if you are not!
You: Why should I care if you smack me in the

mouth?

Me: · • Wallop!

Or more rationally...

Me: Why ought I to be unselfish?

You: It's not a question of 'ought' or being 'unselfish', it's a question of finding an acceptable balance between what is good for me and what is good for those who are 'not-me', while taking into account that I am classed as 'not-me' by every other living individual.

Me: You mean I can be selfish?

You: Selfish actions aren't necessarily bad for others. It depends on the circumstances, right?

The Argument from He Said She Said has little real value because you can make it 'prove' whatever you want. Certainly it's a useful device for persuading others to see things in a particular way, but it's also good to be aware of it when it is being used on you.

You may have noticed that some of the things we have looked at occur in a single sentence or paragraph, while others reveal themselves only when two items separated by many pages are compared, as in the Argument from Double Standards. Now we will look at something which occurs over several successive pages, and to maintain the colour theme of this chapter I will compare it with 'greening' - the process of transforming an environment by changing elements within it until it meets the criteria for being environmentally friendly, or green. I could call it the Argument from Greening, but in this particular case I will call it the Argument from Creeping Capitals (because it's more catchy). It goes like this:

❝ ...some kind of Law or Rule of fair play or decent behaviour or morality or whatever you like to call it... (p8)

❝ ...the human idea of decent behaviour... (p9)

❝ ...a Law of Nature or decent behaviour... (p9)

❝ ...we believe in the Law of Nature. If we do not believe in decent behaviour... (p10)

❝ ...Law of Human Nature, or Moral Law, or Rule of Decent Behaviour... (p10)

❝ ...the Rule of Decent Behaviour... (p12)

❝ ...the Rule of Decent Behaviour... (p12 - 2nd instance)

❝ But if you turn to the Law of Human Nature, the Law of Decent Behaviour, it is a different matter. (p13)

If you haven't spotted it, look at how "decent behaviour" starts out on page 8 with nothing to differentiate it from regular text. It remains unadorned on page 9 but is, for the first time, expressed as an equivalent of "a Law of Nature" - a precursor to the actual transformation. This occurs on page 10 when it not only becomes capitalised but also becomes a "Rule", further reinforced by repetition on page 12. Finally, on page 13, the transformation is complete and it becomes "the Law of Decent Behaviour" which is presented as synonymous with "the Law of Human Nature". From nothing special to a "Law" over the course of six pages.

Now it may well be that Lewis developed his argument in the text which surrounds the highlighted snippets, and the Creeping Capitals are simply a reflection of that development. You can, of course, read it, and decide that for yourself. But whatever you decide, the Argument from Creeping Capitals has the potential to nudge the reader towards the conclusion that the argument has been successfully made whether it actually has or not.

While we are in the area, I'll mention that Page 8 is the first page of Book One of Mere Christianity (pages 1 to 7 comprising the Frontispiece, Forward, and Preface). I don't know how much significance should be attached to it, but the very first words of the book proper - the title of Book One - are an example of a fallacy which goes by the name of Begging The Question. Somewhat amusingly, Begging The Question turns out to be a mistranslation of the Latin *petitio principii*, "assuming the initial point"[3], but let's not get sidetracked by amusing trivia just now.

The title of Book One is as follows:

❝ Right And Wrong As A Clue To The Meaning Of The Universe

If it's not clear to you how that is "begging the question" then you are not the only one. But if we ask "what is the 'initial point' which is being assumed" then it is easier to see that it is "The Meaning Of The Universe", in as much as it assumes the universe has a meaning rather than no meaning at all.

We will never know if Lewis was aware of what he did, but in the vernacular (I like to squeeze that word in if I can - it's so descriptive just in the way it sounds), one might say, "It's a set-up! The whole thing's rigged from the start! He's just trying to pull a fast one using loaded dice!", and, of course, one might be right.

Out in the real world a question which has been put to me on quite a few occasions is this: "Do you believe in God?"

Perhaps 'Begging The Answer' would have been a more descriptive mistranslation than 'Begging The Question' because that's pretty much what is going on here. It's a combination of "assuming the initial point", the Argument from Either Or, and Equivocation. It assumes not only that gods exist but that there is just one of them, while at the same time implying that 'yes' or 'no' are the only possible answers. The equivocation comes in via the words "believe in". It allows the answer "no" to be interpreted to mean "I reject God" rather than "I don't think God exists", in a similar way to how "I don't believe in hitting children" means I reject the practice of hitting children rather than I don't think it ever happens. Good going for an apparently simple five-word question.

I like 'Begging The Answer' so that's what I'll call it: the Argument from Begging The Answer. Will you read the next chapter now?

Reference Links for Chapter 6

1 How Green Was My Valley: http://goo.gl/RWya69

2 Bertrand Russell: http://goo.gl/LZFZrQ

3 Begging The Question: http://goo.gl/sxwDnr

Chapter 7 • There Is No Chapter 7

Oh yes there is!

Oh no there isn't!!

Oh yes there is!!!

And that's the Argument from Pantomime!

If you are not familiar with pantomime, Wikipedia had a good description when I last read the article there[1]. Briefly, pantomime is a musical comedy stage production in which the Comic Lead often instigates a type of "call and response" with the audience, as part of his role, where he says one thing and the audience traditionally says the opposite. For example, if he says "Oh no it isn't!" then the audience replies "Oh yes it is!" and so on.

Another aspect of 'panto' is that it is an exaggerated, larger-than-life presentation where the players are like caricatures, something similar to the way characters in those old black and white cartoons were presented[2], but in living, breathing colour. Their exaggerated behaviour is supposed to make it obvious to everyone, including children, what the message is.

To spot an Argument from Pantomime in the written word requires a bit of imagination. Take this from page 46:

" We have been told, till one is sick of hearing it, that sexual desire is in the same state as any of our other natural desires and that if only we abandon the silly old Victorian idea of hushing it up, everything in the garden will be lovely. It is not true. The moment you look at the facts, and away from the propaganda, you see that it is not.

All together now, "Oh yes it is!"

And again on page 46:

" I know some muddle-headed Christians have talked as if Christianity thought that sex, or the body, or pleasure, were bad in themselves. But they were wrong. Christianity is almost the only one of the great religions which thoroughly approves of the body...

We are allowed to interrupt: "Oh no it's not!"

Another tradition in pantomime is that the villain (there's always a villain) will appear on the stage behind the hero, obviously intent on carrying out some dastardly deed, while the hero apparently has no idea the villain is there. It is the duty of the audience to shout "behind you!" to alert the hero to the danger. Equally traditional is that the hero either appears oblivious to the shouted warning, or feigns deafness, which is the signal for the audience to shout louder.

So here we go: "Behind you!"

The villain of the piece you are currently reading goes by the name of the Argument from Pantomime, and you, of course, are the hero. I told you there is no Chapter 7, but would you listen!? What else can I do but shout "behind you!" (once more, with feeling) very loudly in your inner ear?

Reference Links for Chapter 7

1 Pantomime: http://goo.gl/aLM5Wp
2 Cartoon: http://goo.gl/kBMHVp

Chapter 8 • Razor's Edge

Sorry about Chapter 7. It was all Brian G. Templeford's fault - he told me to do it. Actually I threw it in there just to make sure you hadn't fallen into that torporous state which sometimes overcomes me when I'm reading. You know that state, right? The one in which you're processing the words with your eyes and nodding along, while your comprehension and critical thinking circuits sit idly by, twiddling their thumbs - I hope I'm not the only one who experiences that?

On the assumption that I am not, it raises the question of why and how it happens. It isn't always exactly the same though, at least not for me. Sometimes it's pretty obvious that I'm tired and my brain has become incapable of functioning at its usual level. Other times I get distracted by something, perhaps a snippet of what I'm reading, or something external like a bird's song, or something internal in the back of my mind, and the focus of my attention is split between it and the words on the page. Sometimes it's because what I'm reading is exquisitely badly written or mind-numbingly boring.

An example of a badly written piece is a sentence which, although starting out in a simple, easily understandable and succinct way, meanders so much during the course of its journey, occasionally venturing into side streams of little relevance to the main flow which, although possibly of interest in their own right, serve only as insipient distractions, until, finally, after a series of ponderous excursions into comma separated displays of stigmeological excess, coupled with univocal tokens of simphobia, one finds oneself nearing the end of a paragraph-length sentence of many parts, needlessly overtaxed and quite likely none the wiser regarding its raison d'être, and with question marks regarding what some of it actually means.

I think one example is enough.

Incidentally, in case you are curious about 'stigmeological excess' and 'simphobia', stigmeology is the art of punctuation, and simphobia is fear of speaking straightforwardly and/or using simple terms. To Lewis's credit, his writing in Mere Christianity is, on the whole, quite straightforward, even when dealing with complicated issues. However, examination of his explanations of complicated issues marks him as a man who didn't put much stock in the ideas of William of Ockham¹.

Dear old William is commonly credited with formulating, way back in medieval times, what has become known as Occam's Razor. It's called a 'razor' because it advocates cutting away unnecessary stuff when formulating explanations of anything. As an exaggerated example, if you came home to find a parcel on your doorstep you could explain it by positing that the postman was abducted by aliens, taken to their spaceship where he was forcibly cloned, and the clone was then guided by them to leave the parcel on your doorstep, while the original postman endured numerous intrusive examinations by the aliens. Alternatively, you could cut away all the unnecessary stuff (or not add it in the first place) and go with the simple explanation that the postman left it there.

The principle of Occam's Razor is that a less complicated explanation of something is preferable if it fully explains whatever that 'something' is. Something similar had in fact been formulated before. Thomas Aquinas said in his *Summa Theologica*, a few generations earlier: "it is superfluous to suppose that what can be accounted for by a few principles has been produced by many". However, he used this principle to construct an objection to the Christian god's existence, only to attempt to knock it down with a refutation using an argument based on causality. So Ockham is our man.

On page 24, Lewis wrote about 'dualism', which he described in this way:

> **❝** Dualism means the belief that there are two equal and independent powers at the back of everything, one of them good and the other bad, and that this universe is the battlefield in which they fight out an endless war.

As part of his rebuttal of dualism, he wrote the following:

> **❝** ... So we must mean that one of the two powers is actually wrong and the other actually right.
>
> But the moment you say that, you are putting into the universe a third thing in addition to the two Powers: some law or standard or rule of good which one of the powers conforms to and the other fails to conform to.

Rather than use Occam's Razor to discard the idea of the "third thing" as unnecessary, Lewis went on to do the opposite, asserting that the third thing, which moments before he said 'you' put into the universe, wasn't actually put there by you at all:

> **❝** But since the two powers are judged by this standard, then this standard, or the Being who made this standard, is farther back and higher up than either of them, and He will be the real God.

He could just as easily have used Occam's Razor to give dualism a clean shave (chuckle-haha) by stating that what we humans perceive as 'good' and 'bad' in the universe are not entities in their own right, 'powers', but manifestations of 'perceived behaviour' which if caused or carried out by a human would be met either with commendation or condemnation by other humans.

But of course that would not have served Lewis's purpose. Rather than cut dualism down to size with Occam's Razor, he used dualism as a stepping stone to assert the existence, and total supremacy, of the Christian god. Then, at the same time, he tried to discard the notion of the two 'powers' of dualism, and went to some trouble to achieve this over the course of a couple of pages.

As an aside, something else caught my eye:

> **"** In fact, what we meant by calling them good and bad turns out to be that one of them is in a right relation to the real ultimate God and the other in a wrong relation to Him.
>
> The same point can be made in a different way. If Dualism is true, then the bad Power *must be* a being who likes badness for its own sake. (p24 - my emphasis)

It's the Argument from Must Be, the 'heartless uncle'[2] of the Argument from Either Or. There is of course no reason why the "bad Power" must be "a being who likes badness for its own sake". It could just as easily be "the embodiment of evil" with no concept of liking or disliking anything.

Back to Occam's Razor.

We should not be unduly surprised that Lewis made no

mention of it because Mere Christianity is nearer a piece of propaganda than it is a balanced review of the case for Christianity, and as previously pointed out, even the title of the very first book (of the four which make up Mere Christianity) employed the Argument from Begging The Answer: Right And Wrong As A Clue To The Meaning Of The Universe.

It seems highly unlikely that Lewis, an educated man, was unaware of Occam's Razor, which generates the amusing thought that he was aware of it and employed it, after a fashion, to exclude any mention of it in his book, on the grounds that it was an unnecessary addition to his reasoning. Having read what he wrote, though, I think it more likely he was of the opinion held by some that Occam's Razor is too extreme, and not applicable in all circumstances. Indeed, Walter Chatton, a contemporary of Ockham, devised an 'anti-razor': "If three things are not enough to verify an affirmative proposition about things, a fourth must be added, and so on". I don't know about 'anti-razor', it seems more like a recipe for endless 'woo'.[3]

Be that as it may, it's worth remembering that the book Mere Christianity was compiled from a series of radio broadcasts which Lewis made during World War Two at a time when Britain was under attack and men were needed to fight, and the morale of their families was crucial. Radio was the 'mass media' of the time, the only type of 'real time mass communication' to have invaded the homes of ordinary people up to that point (television was just a flickering dream). It represented an ideal channel for boosting the morale of the nation.

To get a flavour of the time, here's the transcript of a radio broadcast 'to the nation' made by Winston Churchill in his capacity as Prime Minister in June 1940:

❝ I have, myself, full confidence that if all do their duty, if nothing is neglected, and if the best arrangements are made, as they are being made, we shall prove ourselves once again able to defend our Island home, to ride out the storm of war, and to outlive the menace of tyranny, if necessary for years, if necessary alone.

At any rate, that is what we are going to try to do. That is the resolve of His Majesty's Government - every man of them. That is the will of Parliament and the nation.

The British Empire and the French Republic, linked together in their cause and in their need, will defend to the death their native soil, aiding each other like good comrades to the utmost of their strength.

Even though large tracts of Europe and many old and famous States have fallen or may fall into the grip of the Gestapo and all the odious apparatus of Nazi rule, we shall not flag or fail.

We shall go on to the end, we shall fight in France, we shall fight on the seas and oceans, we shall fight with growing confidence and growing strength in the air, we shall defend our Island, whatever the cost may be, we shall fight on the beaches, we shall fight on the landing grounds, we shall fight in the fields and in the streets, we shall fight in the hills; we shall never surrender, and even if, which I do not for a moment believe, this Island or a large part of it were subjugated and starving, then our Empire beyond the seas, armed and guarded by the British Fleet, would carry on the struggle, until, in God's good time, the New World, with all its power and might, steps forth to the rescue and the liberation of the old.

The first of Lewis's multiple wartime radio broadcasts, which together later became Mere Christianity, was transmitted in August 1941. I am fortunate never to have lived in a country at war, and consequently it's hard to imagine the state of mind of people subjected to such conditions day after day, week after week. That said, it's not so hard to imagine that many of those living in wartime Britain were quite likely in a frame of mind which was open to an authoritative voice explaining what was happening in universal terms of "right and wrong" (the name given to Lewis's first four talks), and then, later on, providing something supernal[4] to think about rather than the awful events occurring in the real world around them.

With that perspective, perhaps it's not so surprising that, for his wartime radio talks, Lewis adopted the mantle of King of the Bald Assertion, and shunned Occam's Razor in favour of Chatton's anti-razor approach. What does puzzle me is how the book, published as a single entity several years after the war ended, has achieved such a high status as a work of Christian apologetics. It's chock-full of Bald Assertions and faulty reasoning, some of which we've identified in the previous chapters.

Now it would be unrealistic to expect a book dealing with gods, 'human nature', and the universe not to contain any bald assertions[5] or analogies-which-don't-quite-work, but there is a kind of tipping-point, or razor's edge, past which such things become increasingly difficult to ignore. While it is sometimes justifiable to ignore a few errors in a book because it is not typical of the author's writing, if there are more than a few there comes a point when one has to conclude that it IS typical, and the value of the book is weighed accordingly.

In case you think I am being unfair, below are the results of a little test I did, something it seems Lewis would have approved of according to what he wrote on page 45:

> **❝** ... if, in some strange land, we found that similar acts with mutton chops were popular, one of the possible explanations which would occur to me would be famine. But the next step would be to test our hypothesis by finding out whether, in fact, much or little food was being consumed in that country.

The hypothesis I tested was that if I chose ten pages at random I would find an example of what I've been writing about on each and every one of them. I used the Random Integer Generator at Random.Org[6] to get the ten page numbers and here's what I found (page numbers sorted in ascending order):

Page 21

1 ... a God who takes sides, who loves love and hates hatred ... [Soft Paradox - a being which hates hatred would have to hate itself for its hatred of hatred]

Page 30

1 Laying down your arms, surrendering, saying you are sorry, realising that you have been on the wrong track and getting ready to start life over again from the ground floor - that is the only way out of a "hole". [Bald Assertion/Argument from Only Way - a variation on the Argument from Must Be]

Page 33

1 God never meant man to be a purely spiritual creature. [Bald Assertion]

2 We may think this rather crude and unspiritual. God does not: He invented eating. He likes matter. He invented it. [Bald Assertion x 4]

3 God will invade. [Bald Assertion]

Page 34

1 God is holding back to give us that chance. It will not last for ever. We must take it or leave it. [Bald Assertion x 2. Argument from Either Or]

2 In reality, moral rules are directions for running the human machine. [Bald Assertion]

Page 45

1 One man may eat enough for two, but he does not eat enough for ten. The appetite goes a little beyond its biological purpose, but not enormously. But if a healthy young man indulged his sexual appetite whenever he felt inclined, and if each act produced a baby, then in ten years he might easily populate a small village. This appetite is in ludicrous and preposterous excess of its function. [Bald Assertion x 3. Argument from Wild Conjecture]

Page 70

1 … but if it were true, what it tells us would be bound to be difficult - at least as difficult as modern Physics, and for the same reason. [Bald Assertion]

2 Now the point in Christianity which gives us the greatest shock is the statement that by attaching ourselves to Christ, we can "become Sons of God." [Bald Assertion]

Page 71

1 We are thinking about something that happened before Nature was created at all, before time began. [Hard

Paradox]

2 The intense activity and fertility of the insects, for example, is a first dim resemblance to the unceasing activity and the creativeness of God. [Bald Assertion/Argument from Wild Conjecture]

Page 74

1 This definition is not something we have made up; Theology is, in a sense, experimental knowledge. It is the simple religions that are the made-up ones. [Bald Assertion x 2]

2 And, in fact, He shows much more of Himself to some people than to others - not because He has favourites, but because it is impossible for Him to show Himself to a man whose whole mind and character are in the wrong condition. [Bald Assertion x 3]

3 God can show Himself as He really is only to real men ... For that is what God meant humanity to be like ... [Bald Assertion x 2]

Page 79

1 What grows out of the joint life of the Father and Son is a real Person, is in fact the Third of the three Persons who are God. [Bald Assertion x 2]

2 There is no other way to the happiness for which we were made. [Bald Assertion/Begging The Answer x 2 - assumes we were made, and that we were made for a purpose]

3 They are a great fountain of energy and beauty spurting up at the very centre of reality. [Bald Assertion]

Page 86

1 But I cannot, by direct moral effort, give myself new motives. [Bald Assertion]

2 We then admit that something else, call it "morality" or "decent behaviour," or "the good of society" has claims on this self: claims which interfere with its own desires. [Bald Assertion]

You might have noticed that some of the items listed above also featured in previous chapters, but rest assured they are not repeated here for any other reason than they appear on the pages selected by the Random Number Generator. You are of course at liberty to repeat the test with a new set of page numbers - use the URL in the Reference Links section at the end of this chapter to get a set of page numbers using the exact criteria I used. For me, though, the above results are sufficient to place Mere Christianity in the territory beyond the tipping point I mentioned earlier.

Now it might be said that the alleged Bald Assertions were simply Lewis expressing his opinion. But this is belied in two ways. Firstly by his copious use of the words 'in fact' (twice in the above list and 53 times in the book - a book of less than 100 pages), and secondly by the fact that he explicitly stated he was guessing on at least three occasions:

" But that is guesswork. (p80)

" But of course all this is guesswork. (p82)

" But I do not know: it is only a guess. (p88)

My guess is that Lewis did not share my opinion that the presentation of opinions or beliefs as facts is the bane of our time.

Notes and Reference Links for Chapter 8

1 Occam's Razor: http://goo.gl/KPijtN

2 Heartless Uncle: http://goo.gl/anmTdW

3 Woo: http://skepdic.com/woowoo.html

4 Supernal
     i: of or from the world of the divine; celestial
     ii: of or emanating from above or from the sky

5 Lewis did define theology as "the science of God" (p69) but Mere Christianity is not a scientific paper which would require source references for its all its assertions.

6 Random Numbers: http://goo.gl/NzigD7
  (Please note you will NOT get the same set of numbers I did)

Chapter 9 • Pop Goes The Weasel

“ Facts are stubborn things; and whatever may be our wishes, our inclinations, or the dictates of our passion, they cannot alter the state of facts and evidence. - John Adams (2nd President of the USA)

True, but wishes, inclinations and passions can be, and often are, powerful motivations to misrepresent the facts, skew the evidence, and thereby alter people's perceptions of the facts. About two hundred or so years and forty-one Presidents later, the soon-to-be 44th President, Barack Obama, made the following comment in an interview[1]:

“ And I, you know, I quote in the book one of my favorite stories from the Senate when Daniel Patrick Moynihan of New York is in an argument with a colleague on the floor, and the colleague's probably not doing too well in that argument, Pat Moynihan was a pretty smart guy, and at some point, the other senator gets frustrated and says, "Well, you know what, Pat? You're just entitled to your own opinion and I'm entitled to mine."

And, and Moynihan, frostily I—I'm sure, says, "You are entitled to your opinion, but you're not entitled to your own facts."

True again, but observation suggests that 'entitlement' probably has as much, or as little, influence on people's tendency to misrepresent the facts and skew the evidence today as it did two hundred years ago.

Entitlement is no match for bias. This is true not only in people who put forward their version (or vision) of the facts, but also in people who hear only what they want to hear and allow their assessment of what is said to be influenced by their opinion of the speaker. I notice it in myself when reading quotes; if I read the quote without any knowledge of who it came from, I sometimes find myself changing how I feel about what was said when I see who said it. Of course, I slap myself severely when I catch myself doing it, but that doesn't cure the tendency.

Just for fun, try these quotes on for size. Any idea who I am quoting?

1 *"There were a thousand or more things which I inwardly loved or which I came to love during the course of my stay."*

2 *"... experience teaches that the human being fights only for something in which he believes and which he loves."*

3 *"I can fight only for something that I love."*

4 *"Manliness consists not in bluff, bravado or lordliness. It consists in daring to do right and facing consequences, whether it is in matters social, political or other. It consists in deeds not in words."*

5 *"Those who say religion has nothing to do with politics do not know what religion means."*

So, who said those things? Do you agree with the expressed sentiments? All of them? Some of them? None of them? What kind of people would say those things?

Here are some possibilities:

The Dalai Lama
Napoleon Bonaparte
Marcus Aurelius
Mao Zedong
Mahatma Gandhi
L. Ron Hubbard

Kahlil Gibran
Ho Chi Minh
Franklin D. Roosevelt
Che Guevara
Adolf Hitler
Abraham Lincoln

Okay..time's up! Who do you choose?

The first three came from Mahatma Gandhi. Look at them again and you'll be able to feel his gentle philosophy permeating his words:

1 *"There were a thousand or more things which I inwardly loved or which I came to love during the course of my stay."*

2 *"... experience teaches that the human being fights only for something in which he believes and which he loves."*

3 *"I can fight only for something that I love."*

The remaining two quotes are from Adolf Hitler, and reading his words again, you can't help but feel his arrogance and contempt for 'lesser mortals':

4 *"Manliness consists not in bluff, bravado or lordliness. It consists in daring to do right and facing consequences, whether it is in matters social, political or other. It consists in deeds not in words."*

5 *"Those who say religion has nothing to do with politics do not know what religion means."*

Except, of course, as you really should have learnt from Chapter 2, it is unwise to trust what I write, especially if it involves quotes. It's the other way around. The first three quotes are taken from Hitler's Mein Kampf[2], and the last two are from the Collected Works of Mahatma Gandhi (Volume 44)[3].

Well, that WAS fun, wasn't it! You probably saw right away that I was playing another game even if you had never come across any of the quotes before. Obviously I selected atypical quotes to increase the chances of success for my little ruse, and I also set you up with my comments prior to reading the quotes a second time, but the point I was making is that we are more receptive of something somebody says if we like or admire the person who says it, believing it to be sincere and worthy of respect, and, conversely, more dismissive of something said by someone we dislike.

Assuming you categorise Hitler as a bad or evil man, to hear him talking about love is quite challenging. Can 'evil' people love? I'll come back to that. First we need to think about 'the problem of evil'. But not *that* 'problem of evil' (the one which has exercised the minds of many great thinkers over the last few thousand years). Besides, for my money Epicurus[4] put his opponents in a pickle a long time ago and his argument still has a lot of bite. Be that as it may, the problem of evil I'm referring to is the use of the word 'evil' itself.

'Good' and 'evil' are words often used to describe the two qualities which represent opposite ends of a spectrum. However, in a similar way, there is also the pairing of opposites in the form of the words 'good' and 'bad'. So what is the difference between 'bad' and 'evil'? And is the 'good' which is opposite to 'bad' the same as the 'good' which is opposite to 'evil'?

From how they are used in everyday speech and writing it can seem as if there really are two different spectrums, one for 'good ↔ bad' and one for 'good ↔ evil'. However, to accommodate 'good', 'bad' and 'evil' on one single spectrum it is only necessary to divide it into two halves, with everything on one side of the centre point 'good' and everything on the other side 'bad'. 'Evil' simply occupies the part of the 'bad' side which is furthest from 'good'. It is not important for our present purposes exactly where the threshold from 'bad' to 'evil' lies. It's the nature of that threshold I want to look at.

If we think of how people are described in broad brush terms, then some of them are 'good' and some of them are 'bad'. We tend not to worry about the 'good' people, and consequently it's the 'bad' ones which are often the focus of our attention. The side of the scale the 'bad' people are on is often visualised as a 'slippery slope', a slope which gets progressively steeper the further it gets from the 'good' side. As the slope gets steeper, there comes a 'point of no return' where the slope is so steep that the 'bad' people can do nothing but plummet into the 'depths of evil'. And that is the threshold between 'bad' and 'evil'. 'Evil' people are 'off the scale', sometimes characterised as having fallen, or leapt, into a pit from which there is no way back. Some pity is felt for those who are perceived as having fallen, but only contempt for the alleged leapers.

'Evil' doesn't have an equivalent word on the 'good' side of the scale. 'Evil' is in a special and unique category of its own. I have seen 'saintly', 'holy', 'angelic', and even 'God' put forward as opposites for 'evil', but we have 'unsaintly', 'unholy', 'demonic' and 'Devil' as antonyms of those words, none of which mean quite the same thing as 'evil'. Perhaps it's because nobody really believes that anyone can attain 'ultimate goodness' in the way it is believed that people can be 'evil' ('ultimate badness').

Here's a graphic representation of a 'good - bad - evil' scale.

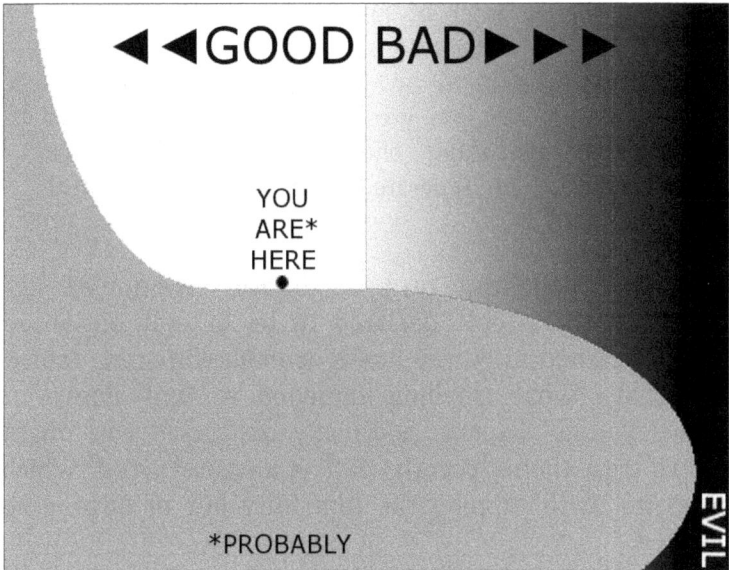

I took the liberty of placing you roughly where I would place myself, and where I suspect that most people would place themselves; not outstandingly 'good', but definitely not 'bad'. However, let's not get caught up with whether this scale is a true representation of the relationship between 'good', 'bad', and 'evil', nor where we fit within it. It's all just for fun.

Except, of course, labelling someone as 'evil' is, all too often, nowhere near a case of being just for fun, but rather a method of 'ultra-othering'. Here's an example as reported in the section of biblestudents.net entitled "Food For Thinking Jehovah's Witnesses"[5]:

❝ The Society claiming to be 'The Faithful and Wise Slave Class' denounced all independent Bible Students

74

outside of the Society as 'The Evil Slave Class'. The Watchtower of June 15, 1987, had this to say:

> By the summer of 1918 ... At the time of the Society's conventions that summer, some apostates turned away and formed their own opposing religious groups. Manifesting the traits of an 'evil slave', they were 'winnowed' like 'chaff' to be separated from Jehovah's faithful remnant.

With that delightful turn of phrase, "winnowed like chaff", all the people declared to be in that out-group were discarded as empty husks, worthless matter, refuse. And that's what labelling someone as 'evil' does - it allows you to dispense with any obligation you might feel to treat them decently. 'Evil' is a weasel word[6] which bares its teeth, ripping the humanity out of anyone so labelled.

But, you might object, that's a rather exaggerated description for what amounts to nothing more than a bit of name calling. And if that was the end of it you would be right. It is also true that although Lewis did make some disparaging comments in Mere Christianity about people who do not share his beliefs, he did not resort to labelling them 'evil'. In fact, he only used the word 'evil' fourteen times in total and it doesn't appear in Book One at all. All the same, he did write about 'witches', people who are frequently labelled as 'evil':

❝ ... if we really thought that there were people going about who had sold themselves to the devil and received supernatural powers from him in return and were using these powers to kill their neighbours or drive them mad or bring bad weather, surely we would all agree that if anyone deserved the death penalty, then these filthy quislings did. (p13)

You probably picked up on the fact that Lewis included "bringing bad weather" alongside "killing" and "driving people mad" as something which deserves the death penalty. Whether you think *any* of those things warrant the death penalty is not the issue. The point is it's an example of how normal criteria for judging someone's actions go out the window when the 'someone' is categorised as 'evil'. Even relatively minor offences are treated as abominations.

In many cases there does not even need to be a real offence at all, the evidence for which can be easily found. A book I recommend for a balanced presentation of times past, and how the label 'evil' was applied, is *A History of the Warfare Of Science With Theology in Christendom*, by Andrew Dickson White. It's a big book (around 900 pages), but then it does deal in quite some detail with a long period of history. It was published in 1896, and therefore includes some antiquated ideas of the time, but nevertheless it presents historical events clearly with copious references to validate the claims. It's available from that well known 'South American' bookstore[7], but one of the relevant sections, *The Agency of Witches*, (and the entire book, for that matter) can be read online[8].

Sadly, labelling someone as 'evil', or alternatively 'possessed by the devil', is not a relic of the past. It is still employed today, and in some places the consequences of being so labelled are as dire as they ever have been. In parts of Africa, children suffer, and some have been killed, as a result of it[9].

To his credit, despite his "bringing bad weather" slip up, Lewis only used the word 'evil' to refer to what he called a Dark Power, never as a label to apply to a person, nor even to the Nazis as a group. What he did do was to use a dismissive, condescending style. His comment on atheism and what he called "Christianity and water", on page 23, is a fine example:

" Both these are boys' philosophies.

Ouch! Clever put-down Mr Lewis! But not clever enough to disguise its weasel nature. Have no fear, though, we can ferret out the truth.

In Chapter 8 I asserted that Mere Christianity is near to being a piece of propaganda. I was wrong. It is not 'near to' being a piece of propaganda at all. It is a fully fledged, paid up, all singing, all dancing piece of propaganda. And if you have read Mere Christianity and that assertion ruffles your feathers, then that is, in itself, proof that the propaganda was powerful, and successful to boot.

In keeping with the style of this book, it is now my duty to point out that the last sentence of the previous paragraph is an example of the sort of technique Lewis made use of to attempt to force his readers into the box he was defining. Here's an example from Book One, Chapter Two:

" I conclude then, that though the differences between people's ideas of Decent Behaviour often make you suspect that there is no real natural Law of Behaviour at all, yet the things we are bound to think about these differences really prove just the opposite. (p12)

The notable thing about that sentence is that as a 'conclusion' it is extremely ill-defined. What are these *things* which we are bound to think which allegedly prove that what we often suspect is wrong? Perhaps they were well defined in the preceding paragraphs? There is this statement made several paragraphs previously, on page 10:

> **"** First ... human beings, all over the earth, have this curious idea that they ought to behave in a certain way, and cannot really get rid of it. Secondly, that they do not in fact behave in that way. They know the Law of Nature; they break it. These two facts are the foundation of all clear thinking about ourselves and the universe we live in.

Lewis packed those few sentences to the brim. From the observation that humans clearly don't always behave in the way they expect other humans to behave, he unilaterally promoted those expectations to the status of an external 'Law', grandiosely going on to make the overblown claim that these alleged 'facts' (that there is a 'Law' and humans 'break' it) are the foundation of *all* clear thinking about pretty much everything. Not bad going for a short paragraph.

That paragraph was the grand finale of Book One, Chapter One. The 'conclusion' quoted previously is the climax of Chapter Two. Between those paragraphs, in the build up to that conclusion, Lewis attempted to make his foundation firm by providing answers to issues which had been raised to him. A large part of it was taken up with dismissing the idea that what he called the Moral Law is simply the herd instinct which had developed just like all our other instincts. Because I agree with Lewis that what he called the Moral Law is not just an instinct neither of the herd variety nor any other - I find what came further into the chapter more interesting. There he addressed the question, "Isn't what you call the Moral Law just a social convention, something that is put into us by education?"

He answered as follows:

> **"** I think there is a misunderstanding here. The people who ask that question are usually taking it for granted that if we have learned a thing from parents and teachers, then that thing must be merely a human invention. But, of course, that is not so.

Oh. "Of course." Nothing to see here. Move along? Well, not quite. It was at that point that Lewis wrote about the multiplication table and the child who grew up alone on a desert island which was featured in Chapter 3, along with the ternary system of numbers. I don't want to go over that again (read Chapter 3 if you need to remind yourself) so let's move along.

What Lewis moved on to was an attempt to shore up his assertion that the "Law of Human Nature" is a "real truth" which "belongs in the same class as mathematics", putting forward two reasons in support of it. His first reason was the one I quoted in Chapter 3 as an illustration of the Argument From Most People. You might recall it went like this:

> **"** ... though there are differences between the moral ideas of one time or country and those of another, the differences are not really very great - not nearly so great as most people imagine - and you can recognise the same law running through them all ...

It wasn't relevant in Chapter 3, but here I'll point out

that while Lewis glibly made the claim that the same law runs through them all, he didn't specify exactly what that law says, which makes it impossible to dispute.

The second reason he gave for why the "Law of Human Nature" is a "real truth" was considerably more convoluted. He started out by asking a couple of questions:

> **‟** When you think about these differences between the morality of one people and another, do you think that the morality of one people is ever **better** or worse than that of another? Have any of the changes been improvements?

Ignore the bold emphasis I added above (and below). I'll come back to it later. For now, just follow how Lewis developed his argument starting with his two questions above. I suspect we are supposed to answer 'yes' and 'yes', a suspicion which is confirmed by what he wrote next:

> **‟** If not, then of course there could never be any moral progress. Progress means not just changing, but changing for the **better**. If no set of moral ideas were **truer** or **better** than any other, there would be no sense in preferring civilised morality to savage morality, or Christian morality to Nazi morality.

With that he put the questions in a context which makes any answer other than 'yes' unacceptable, and his next step was outright confirmation that 'yes' and 'yes' were the correct answers:

> **‟** In fact, of course, we all do believe that some

80

moralities are **better** than others. We do believe that some of the people who tried to change the moral ideas of their own age were what we would call Reformers or Pioneers - people who understood morality **better** than their neighbours did.

Having established the foundation, he reached the point where he could introduce his actual argument:

❝ Very well then. The moment you say that one set of moral ideas can be **better** than another, you are, in fact, measuring them both by a standard, saying that one of them conforms to that standard more nearly than the other.

Okay. That's not unreasonable. We use standard measures for lots of things. For example, we use the metre as a standard measure to accurately compare the size of one thing with another. Lewis elaborated further:

❝ But the standard that measures two things is something different from either. You are, in fact, comparing them both with some Real Morality, admitting that there is such a thing as a real Right, independent of what people think, and that some people's ideas get nearer to that real Right than others.

Boing!!! Pop goes the weasel!! We've had Real Men[tm] and now we have Real Morality[tm]! Where, pray tell, does one get Real Morality[tm]? I know I can go to a hardware store pretty much anywhere in the world and get a one metre rule, and be confident that it will conform to the same standard as any other which I might buy elsewhere. It will conform to the International System of Units' specification of one metre. However, to the best of my knowledge there is no internationally agreed standard of morality of similar standing.

I feel an urge to invoke the Argument from Pantomime, and shout out my reply to Lewis's claim about what I am "in fact" doing:

"Oh no I'm not!!"

What I am doing is comparing two different sets of moral ideas to my personal idea of what is most moral, and doing so does not in any way constitute an "admission" about the existence of an independent "real Right".

Lewis had a habit of bunging the word 'real' in front of intangible things, and not always capitalised as in Real Morality. He apparently thought that doing so somehow makes them 'real' in the sense of being complete and independent entities.

Let's explore that idea. Think about a real World War One aeroplane, say a Sopwith Camel, and compare it to a real World War Two aeroplane, say a Spitfire. You can justifiably say the Spitfire was better than the Sopwith by pointing out the improvements. You can also imagine an ideal aeroplane and point out that the Spitfire's improved features make it more like that ideal aeroplane than the Sopwith, but that doesn't mean the ideal aeroplane actually exists, or that your idea of the ideal aeroplane matches anyone else's, or that your idea of the ideal aeroplane is even possible.

You could, of course, bung the label Real Aeroplane[tm] on your imaginary ideal aeroplane, but that won't make it any more real. It's just an idea in your head. Nevertheless, you could still go on to legitimately compare your Real Aeroplane[tm] with someone else's version despite the fact that neither of them are actually real, that they exist only in the realm of ideas, invented via imagination.

Similarly we can imagine an ideal morality, which we believe would produce a better world, and measure other ideas of morality against it, but that doesn't make it 'real' in any tangible sense, with an existence independent of our imagination.

Perhaps not surprisingly, Lewis felt the need to bolster his argument:

> **"** Or put it this way. If your moral ideas can be **truer**, and those of the Nazis **less true**, there must be something - some Real Morality - for them to be **true** about.

Not much of a bolster there, just a repetition using different words. Of course, bringing in the Nazis at the time of his original radio talk would probably have evoked an emotional response of the "we're all on the same side here, against those evil Nazis" type. However, he wasn't done yet:

> **"** The reason why your idea of New York can be **truer** or **less true** than mine is that New York is a real place, existing quite apart from what either of us thinks.

Quite so. New York is indeed a real place. Any of us can verify it simply by going there. Which puts it in a different class from the nebulous Real Morality^{tm}. Which in turn makes any comparison between New York and Real Morality^{tm} meaningless. Lewis wisely didn't make that direct comparison, neatly switching from real to imaginary realms:

> **"** If when each of us said "New York" each meant merely

"The town I am imagining in my own head," how could one of us have **truer** ideas than the other? There would be no question of truth or falsehood at all.

Quite so, again. Because if we were each merely imagining a town in our own head, without any reference to a real town like New York, we would have to be pretty weird to claim our imagined town was 'truer' than someone else's imagined town. There would indeed be no question of truth or falsehood. However, that's not to say we would not question if our imagined town was 'better' than someone else's. Wisely, once more, Lewis didn't go there, skipping on to his final point:

> **"** In the same way, if the Rule of Decent Behaviour meant simply "whatever each nation happens to approve," there would be no sense in saying that any one nation had ever been **more correct** in its approval than any other; no sense in saying that the world could ever grow morally **better** or morally worse.

Lewis's claim that what he was about to say was "In the same way" was inaccurate at best. Having previously formulated the argument using the word 'truer' (in the Nazis and New York scenarios) he switched to 'more correct' here, using it as a bridge to get to 'better' (the very concept he wisely omitted before).

But then he did set this sleight of hand up right at the start of his argument where he wrote about no set of moral ideas being "truer or better than any other". I emphasised 'truer' and 'better' wherever they appeared throughout his argument to highlight how his sleight of hand was carried out. If you didn't spot what was going on before, go back and scan through what he wrote and make a mental note of the pattern of his usage of those two words.

Just in case you can't be bothered, and you are prepared to trust me on this occasion, the pattern is this: better, better, truer or better, better, better, better, truer, less true, truer, less true, truer, (more correct), better. Lewis began by using 'better' a couple of times, and then slipped in 'truer or better' (as if 'truer' is a synonym for 'better') before resuming his use of 'better' three more times. The sleight of hand occurs where he switched to using 'truer'. Here it is again, except this time I've reconstructed it using 'better' and 'worse':

" Or put it this way. If your moral ideas can be **better**, and those of the Nazis **worse**, there must be something - some Real Morality - for them to be **better** or **worse** than.

" The reason why your idea of New York can be **better** or **worse** than mine is that New York is a real place, existing quite apart from what either of us thinks.

" If when each of us said "New York" each meant merely "The town I am imagining in my own head," how could one of us have **better** ideas than the other? There would be no question of **better** or **worse** at all.

The first two of those three statements work well enough with either Lewis's original wording or my reconstruction. The third statement is where the trick is exposed because with the substitution it makes no sense, revealing that 'truer' is only superficially a synonym for 'better'.

There were times while reading Mere Christianity that I got a similar feeling to the one I have experienced when talking with someone who employs the Argument from It - Will – Be – Really - Hard - Work - To - Expose - All - The - Inconsistencies - In - My - Arguments - So - You - Might - As - Well - Give - In - Now - Because - Even - If - You - Do - Expose - An - Inconsistency - I - Will - Just - Move - On - To - The - Next - And - When - We - Get - To - The - End - I - Will - Simply - Start - Again - Or - Conjure - Up - A - New - One. And, as another aside, that reminds me of something I recently read which had the title Theologian Chess[10]:

❝ In Theology Chess, the theologian has the entire chessboard to himself and only one piece: God. Whenever the opponent (who has no pieces) asks a question about God, the piece may be moved to a different square in any direction with no restriction on distance. This may be done indefinitely until the questioner gets up and leaves.

But back to Lewis. The passage we have been looking at was one that induced that kind of feeling. While I split it into distinct chunks to aid understanding, the original is one gigantic paragraph of almost 500 words. It contains not only the sleight of hand illustrated above, but other manipulative techniques as well.

For example, did you notice how "Real Morality" performed a quick change between paragraphs to emerge at the end as "the Rule of Decent Behaviour"? Now someone (not you, of course!) might say that pointing that out is just nit-picking, and so it would be if it was the only example of Lewis using different terms to refer to the same thing. However, there are other examples in Mere Christianity of him doing just that. In the next chapter we'll take a look at Lewis's mix-and-match, now-

you-see-it-now-you-don't,   find-the-lady   approach   to
getting you where he wanted you.

Notes and Reference Links for Chapter 9

1 Obama: http://goo.gl/BVWK6a

2 Hitler: http://goo.gl/YzAhs

3 Gandhi: http://goo.gl/cvlpjp

4 Epicurus: http://goo.gl/0fPc5t

5 BibleStudents.net: http://goo.gl/h32vJq

6 "...weasel words are words that suck all the life out of the words next to them, just as a weasel sucks an egg and leaves the shell. If you heft the egg afterward it's as light as a feather, and not very filling when you're hungry, but a basketful of them would make quite a show, and would bamboozle the unwary." - Stewart Chaplin: 'The Stained Glass Political Platform', in the Century Magazine, June, 1900 (page 235).

7 Andrew Dickson White book: http://goo.gl/Aywz3u

8 Witches: http://goo.gl/6zTLcx

9 Africa: http://goo.gl/aVMtK7

10 Chess: http://goo.gl/rZY5Lw

Chapter 9.09 • You've Been Framed

Let me state up front that this chapter has nothing to do with the "delightful, cheeky, lovable" / "irritating, shallow, obnoxious" Jeremy Beadle [delete according to prejudice], presenter of the erstwhile British TV shows *Beadle's About* and later *You've Been Framed. Beadle's About* was a repackaging of *Candid Camera* in which the pranks were set up in conjunction with a friend or relative of the 'victim', and were often quite elaborate. *You've Been Framed* featured video clips sent in by viewers, the sort of clips which can now be found in great quantities on YouTube; people falling over, getting wet, bumping into things, and other accidents of a humorous nature. Indeed you can find plenty of videos from both shows on YouTube, and watching them will, I think, confirm that subtlety and Jeremy Beadle were not close associates. The type of framing he went in for was of the no-holds-barred stitch-up variety.

This chapter is about a more subtle type of framing; the art of constructing the language we use in such a way as to improve the chances that it will be understood in a way which is favourable to us or our objectives, preferably without our target audience realising that any manipulation has taken place. Subtlety is clearly the key, although the end result can still be a stitch-up.

If you've read more than a snippet or two of Mere Christianity then the chances are high that you have been the target of framing. In fact the same applies if you have only read the snippets quoted in this book. But before we look at what Lewis wrote, here's what Wikipedia has to say on the subject of 'framing':

" Framing in communication can be viewed as positive or negative depending on the audience and what kind of information is being presented. Framing might also be understood as being either equivalence frames, which represent logically equivalent alternatives portrayed in different ways [see framing effect (psychology)] or as emphasis frames, which simplify reality by focusing on a subset of relevant aspects of a situation or issue. When discussing framing as an 'equivalence frame', the information being presented is based on the same facts, but the 'frame' in which it is presented changes thus creating a reference dependent perception.

Got that? No? Me neither. While it provides some helpful information, it delves a bit too deeply into a subject which, from the language used, is obviously not a simple one. It presents the information in an academic context, or frame, which requires previous knowledge or subsequent research to fully understand it. In the same way that I said I didn't want to get bogged down with the nomenclature of logical fallacies, I don't want to get hung up on defining what type of frame a piece of text is an example of. Read the Wikipedia article and follow the links there if you want to know the ins and outs of it. Here I will present examples which fall into the broad category of framing.

While it's still fresh in our minds, take another look at this from the previous chapter:

" ... human beings, all over the earth, have this curious idea that they ought to behave in a certain way, and cannot really get rid of it. (p10)

There is no grammatical need for the word 'curious' - the

sentence would make just as much sense without it - so we have to ask what was the purpose of inserting it. There are other adjectives with similar meaning which appear in lists of synonyms for 'curious' - novel, odd, peculiar, strange, unexpected - but none of them would frame the word 'idea' in quite the same way that 'curious' does. It was a clever choice because it implies something special about the 'idea', something you wouldn't quite expect, something mysterious, something which can't quite be explained.

There is one other non-essential word in that sentence: 'really'. What role does it play? What is the difference between "cannot get rid of it" and "cannot really get rid of it"? The 'really' version says to me that even if I think I've got rid of it I will be deceiving myself, that the 'idea' has substance of its own, independent of my thoughts.

Now you might be thinking that this is reading too much into a simple sentence, over-analysing it and picking on insignificant details. As a writer I have to take into account how I think you, the reader, will react to my words while I'm deciding which ones I will use, and consequently I choose my words carefully in an attempt to ~~reduce~~ ~~negate~~ minimise the chances of you ~~objecting to~~ disagreeing with what I write or ~~wilfully misunderstanding it~~ losing the thread. Lewis was a skilled and prolific writer not only of scripts for radio talks but also of books and novels. It would be absurd, despite a few examples where he apparently got it wrong, to think he didn't take great care over his choice of words and phrasing.

In verbal communication the term 'back channel' is generally understood to refer to the nods, grunts, and other usually short responses offered to a speaker by the one listening. I think there is a similar channel which affects writers' communications, but the difference is that writers do not have the luxury of observing the back channel in real time. While a speaker can adjust their presentation on the basis of signals received, writers have to second guess what will happen in the back channel imprisoned in a reader's head.

Whether you are listening to someone or reading what they wrote, the things that drive the back channel still occur in your head. The difference is that in verbal communication situations you have the option to express those things externally through words, sounds, and body language, whereas when you are reading they manifest themselves as an internal conversation in your head, something which might well be happening in your head right now. If I do not control, or at least influence the volume, and contents, of the back channel chat going on in your head then I am in danger of losing you to it (Hey! You there! Pay attention when I'm writing to you!).

In Chapter 7 I made a joke of the Argument from Pantomime because it is not an argument that any wise communicator would invite, let alone instigate. The use of framing words, as in Lewis's sentence above, can help to avoid the possibility of an Argument from Pantomime destroying the flow of thought which the writer is trying to guide in a reader's head. Suppose Lewis had written that sentence without 'curious' or 'really':

❝ ... human beings, all over the earth, have this idea that they ought to behave in a certain way, and cannot get rid of it.

"Oh no they don't! What nonsense!"

Not necessarily the reaction a reader would have, but 'curious' and 'really' frame the sentence in such a way that that reaction is less likely. 'Curious' takes the focus away from the bald assertion, guiding the back channel to consider whether the idea is actually 'curious' rather than some other kind of idea. 'Really' operates in a similar way, and by influencing what's going on in the back channel the chances are increased that the front channel message will be accepted.

Below is the full, monster paragraph we looked at in Chapter 9. The emphasised words and phrases are those I think are pertinent to the topic in hand, and I have also inserted some comments between square brackets:

" There are two reasons for saying it belongs to the same class as mathematics. The first is, **as I said in the first chapter** [so you don't have to pay very close attention because it's already been settled], that though there are differences between the moral ideas of one time or country and those of another, the differences are not **really very** great [practically non-existent so not even worth considering] - not **nearly** so great as **most people** imagine [remember the Argument from Most People? You don't want to be part of the seething mass of silly-know-nothings, do you!] - and you can recognise the same law running through them all: whereas **mere** conventions [that is, things which are nowhere near as 'real' or important as 'laws'], like the rule of the road or the kind of clothes people wear, may differ to any extent. The other reason is this. When you think about these differences between the morality of one people and another, do you think that the morality of one people is **ever** better or worse [let's make the scope for answering 'yes' truly enormous] than that of another? Have any of the changes been improvements? If not, then **of course** [it almost goes without saying so no need to think too deeply about it] there could never be any moral progress. Progress means not just changing, but changing for the better. If no set of moral ideas were truer or better than any other, there would be no sense in preferring **civilised** morality [just setting you up to associate 'civilised' with 'Christian'] to **savage** morality [and, of course, to associate 'savage' with 'Nazi'], or **Christian** ['civilised'] morality to **Nazi** ['savage'] morality. **In fact, of course** [a double helping of no need-to-question-this], we all do **believe** [so much more unquestionable than 'think'] that some moralities are better than others. We do **believe** [no, really, we - and we includes you - don't merely 'think'] that some of the people who tried to change the moral ideas of their own age were what we would call Reformers or Pioneers - people who **understood** morality [not "came up with new ideas about" or "developed" - because, remember, morality is a pre-existing and complete set of external rules] better than their **neighbours** did [let's keep this small-town and friendly]. Very well then. The moment you say that one set of moral ideas can be better than another, you are, **in fact**, [therefore indisputable] measuring them both by a standard, saying that one of them conforms to that standard more nearly than the other. But the standard that measures two things is something different from either. You are, **in fact** [really - a fact is a fact so no reason to query it], comparing them both with some **Real** [tada!] Morality, **admitting** [because you will be guilty, so very, very guilty, if you do otherwise] that there is such a thing as a **real** [tada!] Right, independent of what people think, and that some people's ideas get nearer to that **real** [tada!] Right than others. Or put it this way. If your moral ideas can be truer, and those of the Nazis less true, there must be something - some **Real** [tada!] Morality - for them to be true about. The

94

reason why your idea of New York can be truer or less true than mine is that New York is a **real** [tada!] place, existing quite apart from what either of us thinks. If when each of us said "New York" each meant merely "The town I am imagining in my own head," how could one of us have truer ideas than the other? There would be no question of truth or falsehood at all. **In the same way** [so it must be true], if the Rule of Decent Behaviour meant simply "whatever each **nation** happens to approve" there would be no sense in saying that any one **nation** [nations being similar to cities like New York, just bigger, so the 'in the same way' works better] had ever been more correct in its approval than any other; no sense in saying that the world could ever grow morally better or morally worse.

Okay. That's enough of that! I promise not to feature such a gargantuan example again, but it does serve to illustrate how a reader's back channel can be influenced by the choice of words and phrases. And thinking of how words are used, now might be a good time to recall Lewis's statement which I mentioned at the end of Chapter 1:

“ It is only a question of using words so that we can all understand what is being said.

To put it in context, he was talking about the word 'Christian' and what it means. Although he didn't frame it in such terms, he was making an oblique reference to a fallacy which is sometimes called the 'No True Scotsman' fallacy. Quite why the Scottish have been used to illustrate the fallacy I don't know, but it refers to the assertion that even though a man was born within the borders of Scotland to Scottish parents, because of some specific behaviour or belief he cannot be considered a 'true' Scotsman[2]. For example, "No true Scotsman puts sugar on his porridge!"

Lewis argued against the No True Scotsman fallacy like this:

❝ When a man who accepts the Christian doctrine lives unworthily of it, it is much clearer to say he is a bad Christian than to say he is not a Christian.

Succinctly stated and a good example of "using words so that we can all understand what is being said", in stark contrast to the long, duplicitous paragraph we just looked at. It is also in contrast to much of what he wrote in Mere Christianity, although not always in the same way.

Lewis had no qualms about leaving out, ignoring, or playing down pertinent information. In the very first paragraph of Book One, Chapter One, Lewis argued that the fact that men quarrel proves the existence of "The Law of Human Nature". Rather oddly, he also pointed out that if that 'Law' does not exist then instead of quarrelling they might fight like animals, and then completely ignored the fact that *some* men *do* fight like animals (and the implications that has for his argument regarding the existence of the 'Law'). Instead he took the position that the existence of the 'Law' had been proved, and moved on to build further arguments based on that 'proof'.

As an aside, I would not be at all surprised if someone was to respond to the fact that some men do fight like animals with, "yes, but the exception proves the rule."

However, "the exception proves the rule" doesn't mean

what that someone thinks it does. It doesn't mean that 'any' exception to any rule proves the rule is true (I'm tempted to insert a "Doh!" here). It means that when a rule is expressed as an exception then it implicitly establishes that there *is* a rule to which it is the exception. For example, a sign which says "parking prohibited on Sundays" (the exception) 'proves' that parking *is* allowed on the other six days of the week (the rule)[3].

On page 16 there is an example of leaving out information which, in this case, results in an extraordinary distortion of the truth:

❝ Science works by experiments. It watches how things behave. Every scientific statement in the long run, however complicated it looks, really means something like, "I pointed the telescope to such and such a part of the sky at 2:20 A.M. on January 15th and saw so-and-so," or, "I put some of this stuff in a pot and heated it to such-and-such a temperature and it did so-and-so."

The part he left out was that while science does indeed "watch how things behave", it *works* by making predictions based on those observations, and then testing those predictions. And it's not as if that is, or ever was, a secret. Copernicus published his heliocentric model four hundred years earlier, and it was his predictions regarding the motions of celestial bodies, based on his observations, which made his model revolutionary (Pun? What pun?). That process of discovery, the scientific method, had not been scrapped in the intervening years, so it seems unlikely Lewis was unaware of it.

He did a similar thing on the following page where he wrote:

" If there was a controlling power outside the universe, it could not show itself to us as one of the facts inside the universe - no more than the architect of a house could actually be a wall or staircase or fireplace in that house. The only way in which we could expect it to show itself would be inside ourselves as an influence or a command trying to get us to behave in a certain way.

Here he didn't just omit something relevant, he categorically excluded it. No doubt it has crossed your mind too that the controlling power outside the universe who features in a well-known book of scripture was said to have found plenty of ways to make its presence felt in the real world, ranging from 'personal' appearances in the form of burning bushes and the like, to extravagant waterworks of various dimensions. But then, had Lewis included such things as reasonable expectations his whole argument for the existence of Real Morality™ would have fallen apart, which might explain the omission.

There are a lot of things Lewis either took for granted or didn't think merited an explanation. In Chapter 3 we touched on his use of the capitalised personal pronoun 'He' when referring to the power-which-was-not-yet-a-personal-god, but we didn't ask why he assumed the soon-to-be-defined-as-a-personal-god was male. As we have seen, Lewis's blatantly male-centric views probably mean it was not a question that entered his mind, and therefore was not a candidate for explanation. As a break from analysing his words, let's think about the assumption that a god-like power will be male.

In Lewis's case it's clear that he was talking about the Christian god right from the start and, despite his claims to the contrary, it was that personal god rather than an anonymous power which was in his mind all along. That being the case, it follows that he would automatically consider it to be male because everybody knows that the Christian god is male. But why is it male?

The Greco-Roman pantheon of gods was believed to be a family of many generations which explains the existence of both male and female gods. Familial generations require sexual relations, and sexual relations require appropriate anatomy and gender. That's pretty clear, but before we move on, as a side note (because it wasn't always obvious to me) it's worth remembering that although it is commonly referred to as Greek *mythology* today, the people of the time believed in the reality of their gods just as much as today's worshippers believe in the reality of their god or gods. In fact those ancient folks' beliefs were so strong that in 399 BCE, Socrates, a prominent philosopher, was tried and put to death, one of the charges against him being "failure to acknowledge the gods".

Back on topic, it's not so clear cut as to why the Abrahamic god (the god of Judaism, Christianity, and Islam) is male. What is it that defines someone as male? Is it behaviour or some physical attribute? Surely it has to be a physical attribute - a woman whose behaviour is 'butch' or 'gruff' is not said to 'be' male, she is said to be behaving 'like' a male. If it was behaviour which defined someone as male then a person who behaved like a male, regardless of what type of genitalia they possess, would 'be' male. Plainly (to the naked eye, so to speak) the possession of a penis and its associated bits and pieces is the primary requirement for someone to be classed as male.

Now a Christian could argue that Jesus had a penis (not that it's likely they would, nor that it's actually mentioned anywhere, as far as I know, but it's reasonable to assume he did) and therefore, being one of the three persons of the trinity, it's obvious that the Abrahamic god is male. Ignoring the question of what happened to the divine penis after the ascension, and whether it was ever used in any capacity other than as a liquid waste disposal chute while on Earth, at least the Christians have some wiggle room. Not so for Jews and Muslims. The god of their faiths never materialised in human form, making a penis surplus to requirements.

That's not to say that appearances of the Abrahamic god did not feature in the scriptures; they did. But none of them that I am aware of *required* maleness, most of them being manifestations in the form of columns of fire and suchlike. Even in the case of Jesus, I know of nothing in the scriptures, at least not in those which detail the alleged events of his earthbound life, that demonstrate a *requirement* that he had to be male.

So what are we to make of the fact that the Abrahamic god is by all accounts male? One possible explanation is that this deity, despite not engaging in any sexual activity itself, somehow preferred the idea of being male, and consequently made everything to suit a male point of view. But that seems to be very much like favouritism, at best, or outright discrimination at worst - not an admirable trait in humans, let alone a deity.

Another explanation which might be more plausible is that this deity was invented by human males (using the same mental processes used to invent the characters in novels and short stories) and quite naturally they invented a deity whose sex coincided with their own, and one whose views reflected those prevalent among human males at the time.

Here I would like to remind you that this book is not

about whether gods exist or not. In good Lewisian style I am instructing you to keep any thoughts along those lines out of your head. For our purposes, the 'plausible explanation' merely serves as a model to demonstrate how things which are not intrinsically normal can become accepted as normal, so much so that it never surfaces as something to think about, let alone question, in many people's minds.

So let's just suppose that several thousand years ago your great, great, great (plus several hundred more iterations of 'great') grandfather Alfie and his friends were sitting around relaxing after a long day of manly labour, as men seem inclined to do, and in amongst the chat about why can't the women just leave us alone to relax instead of nagging us to do this, or that, or the other, and why can't they just get on with doing the cooking and looking after the kids, one of the group turned to your ancestor and said, "Yeah, but what's it all about Alfie? I mean the whole shebang. Why are we here and how did we get here?"

Alfie, being the acknowledged leader, and a bit of a thinker too, didn't respond with, "Oh don't start with that crap again, Arnie!" which was the response Arnie had previously received when he'd asked the question of some of the others. Instead the wise old Alfie said, "I've been thinking about that myself, Arnie, and I think I can answer your question. You see, when you think about it, it's obvious really. Someone must have made this place and put us here so that we can sit together to discuss important things like 'why are we here and how did we get here'."

Now that was an engaging answer which caught the attention of the whole group, mainly because they had subconsciously made an association between "discussing important things" and "being important", the implied elevation in status making it very attractive. After further discussion it was agreed that there was no doubt about it, someone special must have made them for some kind of special purpose, even if that special purpose wasn't entirely clear yet. They were so pleased with their conclusion they thought it a good excuse for another round of drinks.

Another sign of your grand-ancestor's wisdom was that he never got as drunk as his companions which allowed him to maintain a slight aloofness, or to put it in more down-to-earth terms, he was able to control his consumption of alcohol so that it never caused his behaviour to deteriorate to the levels of crassness reached by the others. But whichever way it is viewed, it was part of the reason he was considered the leader; he never got as rat-arsed as the rest of them so even when he was drunk he was invariably more articulate than they were. And not surprisingly he used it to his advantage.

However, despite his relative temperance, Alfie was not immune to the effects of alcohol, and was emboldened proportionately. A few sessions later, it was a simple step to claim that in fact he had met the special someone, and the special someone had spoken to him just like they were all speaking together, although it was in a dream. Of course it provoked a few jeers, and even laughter, but when it became clear that Alfie wasn't laughing, more serious questions emerged.

"What was he like?" they asked.

And that assumption that it was a 'he' was how it all started. After all, how could it be anything other than 'he' - it had already been agreed that it was the men who were important so it went without saying, or even thinking about, that someone even more important would have to be a man. Some time later it occurred to Arnie to ask, "Where do the women fit in? I mean, did 'he' make them too?"

After some ribald comments and laughter about it being the men who did the 'fitting in' and how some pitifully endowed men hardly fitted in at all, the mist of silence which enveloped them was eventually dispersed by good old Alfie.

"Women were made for us, for our benefit. 'He' made us first, and then, seeing that we had needs, 'he' made women to service them."

Bingo! The logic was unassailable, especially to a group of drunken men. What's more though, it still seemed very reasonable after the hangovers had subsided the following morning. And when, some days later, Alfie revealed that 'he' had been in touch again and had confirmed the truth of the matter, not only did his status rocket sky high among the men, but also the fate of women was sealed.

Not exactly 'end of story' - it wouldn't take much imagination to extend it down through the ages, and, because we could make it up as we went along, it would probably reflect the changes in our outlook along the way. However, what that stub of a story does show is how, at any given time, our environment and culture frames the way we make assumptions. One other thing it shows is how easy it is to invent characters, put them in an imaginary setting, and breathe 'life' into them by putting words in their mouths.

And, I'm sure you'll be pleased to know, it's not 'end of story' for our investigation of Lewis's use of words either. There's more in the next chapter.

Notes and Reference Links for Chapter 9.09

1 Framing: http://goo.gl/QUUyG6
2 Yet again we find the default person is a man.
3 Exception: http://goo.gl/zwxek4

Chapter 10 • The One After Nine-O-Nine

The rather strange numbering of the previous chapter was merely a contrivance to allow me to make the title of this one what it is. If the title means nothing to you, then I'm happy to tell you it is the title of a song written by John Lennon and performed by The Beatles, a band of some repute in the 1960s. I don't think it's one of their best by any means, but if you are interested you can find out more about it at thebeatles.com website[1]. Please also note that despite the fact that Chapter 1 has the title 'Imagine', which happens to be the title of another somewhat more famous song written by John Lennon, there is no underlying link or special significance in my choice of title for this chapter. It was simply a convenient way to demonstrate contrivance in action.

We have already seen some examples of contrivance in Lewis's writing, although I didn't label them as such. We saw one in Chapter 9 where he contrived to conflate the word 'truer' with the word 'better', allowing him to reach his desired conclusion. There is an abundance of contrivance in Mere Christianity, but not wishing to labour the point I will select only one or two of the most glaring examples, and leave it to you to identify the rest (if you are bold enough to venture through Lewis's writing).

His treatment of science is illustrative. We saw in the previous chapter how he short-changed his readers about how science works, omitting the most important factor. By doing so he was able to show that science was not much good, to use one of his phrases, when it comes to the 'big' questions, to downplay its ability to probe the unknown. A few sentences after the section referred to above, he had this to say:

> **ℂ** The statement that there is any such thing, and the statement that there is no such thing, are neither of them statements that science can make. And real scientists do not usually make them.

As an added bonus, tacked onto the end of that you get a real live example of a No True Scotsman ploy, but let's not dwell on it, nor on the fact that even if science can't make those statements it doesn't follow that any other 'discipline' can.

Those couple of sentences were near the beginning of the book where Lewis was trying to establish there is 'something out there', something with a capital 'S', something 'real' yet undetectable, so there was good reason to avoid the analytical power of science, and its habit of making predictions and generally poking its nose in where it's not wanted. However, during the course of the book, he contrived to restore science's reputation so that he could use it in Book Four to prop up, or underpin, the validity of Theology.

Science's rehabilitation began on page 23 where he enlisted the help of "a scientist" as a trustworthy, knowledgeable source:

> **ℂ** The table I am sitting at looks simple: but ask a scientist to tell you what it is really made of all about the atoms and how the light waves rebound from them and hit my eye and what they do to the optic nerve and what it does to my brain - and, of course, you find that what we call "seeing a table" lands you in mysteries and complications which you can hardly get to the end of.

On page 32 he continued the process, the implication of this statement (with the ones which surround it) being that the "ordinary man" is absolutely justified in accepting the authority of "the scientists":

❝ The ordinary man believes in the Solar System, atoms, evolution, and the circulation of the blood on authority - because the scientists say so.

Lewis also made use of the 'sciencey' word 'technical' to add a measure of factuality to this assertion on page 36:

❝ But it might be absolute hell in a million years: in fact, if Christianity is true, Hell is the precisely correct technical term for what it would be.

And again on page 48, albeit in a less ambiguous context:

❝ ... people often misunderstand what psychology teaches about "repressions." It teaches us that "repressed" sex is dangerous. But "repressed" is here a technical term: it does not mean "suppressed" in the sense of "denied" or "resisted."

Then, on page 69, in the very first paragraph of Book Four, Lewis was able to reveal that Theology *is* science, the rehabilitation complete:

❝ Everyone has warned me not to tell you what I am going to tell you in this last book. They all say "the ordinary reader does not want Theology; give him plain practical religion." I have rejected their advice. I do not think the ordinary reader is such a fool. Theology means "the science of God," and I think any man who wants to think about God at all would like to have the clearest and most accurate ideas about Him which are available. You are not children: why should you be treated like children?

Adopting a somewhat maverick persona, Lewis raised a metaphorical middle finger to "everyone", and defended the "ordinary reader", declaring him to be not only adult but also capable of understanding ... wait for it ... science. Read the book if you want to know what went on inbetween, but on page 74 he reinforced the sciencey nature of Theology several times:

❝ This definition is not something we have made up; Theology is, in a sense, experimental knowledge. It is the simple religions that are the made-up ones. When I say it is an experimental science "in a sense," I mean that it is like the other experimental sciences in some ways, but not in all.

❝ You can put this another way by saying that while in other sciences the instruments you use are things external to yourself (things like microscopes and telescopes), the instrument through which you see God is your whole self.

❝ Christian brotherhood is, so to speak, the technical equipment for this science - the laboratory outfit.

Pretty convincing stuff providing you don't ask too many questions like, say, "how do you calibrate this instrument called 'your whole self'?"

Moving swiftly on, page 75 reveals that Lewis appears to have thought that perhaps he'd overdone the whole science thing and felt it necessary to put it in its place once more:

" It was the Theologians who first started the idea that some things are not in Time at all: later the Philosophers took it over: and now some of the scientists are doing the same.

I can't help wondering if he had to resist the temptation to insert the word 'even' between 'now' and 'some'. But that's just pure speculation, so excuse me for a short time while I stand, shame-faced in the corner of the room, reciting the words of Thomas Henry Huxley (in *The Advance of Science in the Last Half-Century* - 1889*):*

" From the dawn of exact knowledge to the present day, observation, experiment, and speculation have gone hand in hand; and, whenever science has halted or strayed from the right path, it has been, either because its votaries have been content with mere unverified or unverifiable speculation (and this is the commonest case, because observation and experiment are hard work, while speculation is amusing); or it has been, because the accumulation of details of observation has for a time excluded speculation.

Back on point, near the end of the book Lewis returned to the task of putting science in its place:

" Again and again it [the world] has thought Christianity was dying, dying by persecutions from without or corruptions from within, by the rise of Mohammedanism, the rise of the physical sciences, the rise of great anti-Christian revolutionary movements.

But every time the world has been disappointed. (p97)

To sum up, Lewis seemed to view science as if it is a piece of fecal matter: something which is an excellent fertiliser but which needs to be held at arms length while using, whenever possible, the rubber gloves of mathematics to avoid getting soiled. Before we leave the subject of science, I'd like to draw your attention to the one remaining instance of his use of the word 'technical', on page 79:

" This third Person is called, in technical language, the Holy Ghost or the "spirit" of God.

I find myself almost desperate to know what that "third Person" is called in *non-technical* language. If you can help me out with that I would appreciate it no end.

Lewis was not a scientist, but he was very well educated, studying at University College, Oxford. It was there, between 1920 and 1923, that he gained a 'triple first', specifically in Honour Moderations (Greek and Latin Literature), Greats (Philosophy and Ancient History), and English. While such achievements can hardly be described as those of an 'ordinary man', he contrived to present himself as 'ordinary' in Mere Christianity, the first instance of it being in his Preface:

" I am a very ordinary layman of the Church of England, not especially "high", nor especially "low", nor especially anything else ... I should have been out of my depth in such waters [theology or ecclesiastical history]: more in need of help myself than able to help others.

He restated his status as a layman on page 29:

❝ But as I said in the preface to this book, I am only a layman, and at this point we are getting into deep water. I can only tell you, for what it is worth, how I, personally, look at the matter.

His interpretation of telling "only his personal view" consisted largely of making countless bald assertions about the Christian god, including what it consists of, what it likes, dislikes, thinks and wants, and what it did, didn't, can, can't, will and will not do, as if they were incontrovertible facts.

Below is a list I compiled of the statements in his book which not only contain the word 'God' but also are statements about that god. The list does not contain the many similar statements in which the word 'He' features as a substitute for and reference to 'God'. There are 96 items in the list and there is actually no need to read them all. I've reproduced the list here merely to give anyone who wants to find them in Lewis's book the ability to do so. Feel free to skip over the list, although you might like to look at the one I have highlighted which, in my estimation, is a fine example of self-contained contrivance:

❝ God is the only comfort ... (p19)

❝ ... nonsense that is damned is under God's curse, and will (apart from God's grace) ... (p22)

❝ God created things which had free will. (p26)

❝ The happiness which God designs ... (p26)

❝ Of course God knew what would happen ... (p26)

❝ God made us ... (p27)

" Now God designed the human machine to run on Himself. (p27)

" God cannot give us a happiness and peace apart from Himself ... (p27)

" God has landed on this enemy-occupied world ... (p28)

" Remember, this repentance, this willing submission to humiliation and a kind of death, is not something God demands of you before He will take you back ... (p30)

" We love and reason because God loves and reasons ... (p30)

" ... which God, in His own nature, never does at all - to surrender, to suffer, to submit, to die. Nothing in God's nature corresponds to this process at all. (p30)

" God can share only what He has ... (p30)

" You and I can go through this process only if God does it in us; but God can do it only if He becomes man. (p31)

" Now the God who arranged that process is the same God who arranges how the new kind of life - the Christ life - is to be spread. (p31)

" God never meant man to be a purely spiritual creature. (p33)

" We may think this rather crude and unspiritual. God does not: He invented eating. He likes matter. He invented it. (p33)

" God will invade. (p33)

" ... this time it will be God without disguise ... (p33)

" God is holding back to give us that chance. (p34)

" It is, of course, quite true that God will not love you any the less ... (p37)

" God is no fonder of intellectual slackers than of any other slackers. (p37)

" But God is not deceived by externals. (p38)

" ... the deep, strong, unshakable kind of happiness God intends for us. (p39)

" God judges them by their moral choices. (p43)

" But God does not judge him on the raw material at all, but on what he has done with it. (p43)

" Each of them, if he seriously turns to God, can have that twist in the central man straightened out again ... (p44)

" God knows our situation ... (p47)

" Very often what God first helps us towards is ... (p48)

" ... the grace which both parents ask, and receive, from God. (p51)

" God intends us to love all selves ... (p55)

" In God you come up against something which is in every respect immeasurably superior ... (p57)

" ... made (like us) by God ... (p60)

66 ... feelings are not what God principally cares about. (p61)

66 God has been waiting for the moment at which you discover that there is no question of earning a pass mark in this exam ... (p65)

66 Every faculty you have, your power of thinking or of moving your limbs from moment to moment, is given you by God. (p65)

66 When a man has made these two discoveries God can really get to work. (p65)

66 ... what God cares about is ... (p65)

66 God is not like that. (p67)

66 ... God has brought us into existence ... (p70)

66 What God begets is God; just as what man begets is man. What God creates is not God ... (p71)

66 Everything God has made has some likeness to Himself. (p71)

66 Matter is like God in having energy: though, again, of course, physical energy is a different kind of thing from the power of God. (p71)

66 But life, in this biological sense, is not the same as the life there is in God ... (p71)

66 **The intense activity and fertility of the insects, for example, is a first dim resemblance to the unceasing activity and the creativeness of God. (p71)**

" That is not the same thing as the love that exists in God ... (p71)

" When we come to man, the highest of the animals, we get the completest resemblance to God ... (p71)

" But what man, in his natural condition, has not got, is Spiritual life - the higher and different sort of life that exists in God. (p71)

" The Spiritual life which is in God from all eternity ... (p72)

" God begets Christ ... (p72)

" ... what God the Father begets is God ... (p72)

" The whole purpose for which we exist is to be thus taken into the life of God. (p72)

" ... what is prompting him to pray is also God ... (p73)

" God is the thing to which ... (p73)

" God is also the thing inside ... (p73)

" God is also the road ... (p73)

" ... he is being pulled into God, by God ... (p73)

" When you come to knowing God, the initiative lies on His side. (p74)

" ... the instrument through which you see God is your whole self. (p74)

" God can show Himself as He really is only to real men. (p74)

" For that is what God meant humanity to be like ... (p74)

" Almost certainly God is not in Time. (p75)

" God is not hurried along in the Time-stream ... (p76)

" You cannot fit Christ's earthly life in Palestine into any time-relations with His life as God beyond all space and time. (p76)

" But God has no history. (p76)

" God is a Being which contains three Persons while remaining one Being ... (p77)

" Naturally God knows how to describe Himself much better than we know how to describe Him. (p78)

" What grows out of the joint life of the Father and Son is a real Person, is in fact the Third of the three Persons who are God. (p79)

" We are not begotten by God ... (p79)

" The Son of God became a man to enable men to become sons of God. (p80)

" ... what God did about us was this. (p80)

" ... as God sees it, it would not look like ... (p81)

" In the long run God is no one but Himself ... (p81)

" ... God probably never meant them to be that. (82)

" ... who is man (just like you) and God (just like His Father) is actually at your side ... (p84)

" The real Son of God is at your side. (p84)

" ... still as much God as He was when He created the world ... (p85)

" ... everything which really needs to be done in our souls can be done only by God. (p86)

" In reality, of course, it is God who does everything. (p86)

" God looks at you as if you were a little Christ ... (p86)

" God became Man for no other purpose. (p88)

" Because God is forcing him on ... (p90)

" There are people in other religions who are being led by God's secret influence ... (p92)

" ... in God's eyes Dick Firkin needs "saving" ... (p93)

" The niceness, in fact, is God's gift ... (p93)

" ... God has allowed natural causes ... (p93)

" ... that is not, for God, the critical part ... (p93)

" What He is watching and waiting and working for is something that is not easy even for God ... (p93)

" God can see to that part of the problem. (p93)

" Of course God regards a nasty nature as a bad and deplorable thing. (p93)

" The only things we can keep are the things we freely give to God. (p94)

" ... you are at every moment totally dependent on God. (p94)

" God became man to turn creatures into sons ... (p95)

" Century by century God has guided nature ... (p98)

With so many non-trivial bald assertions throughout the book it is no surprise that Lewis attempted to lubricate the passage of his message to his readers' brains. He did it by playing the equality card; that 'you', his reader, and he are actually very alike, birds of a feather, probably "in it together". An "old pals" act of sorts. He established it with quite a flourish, on page 10:

" None of us are really keeping the Law of Nature. If there are any exceptions among you, I apologise to them. They had much better read some other work, for nothing I am going to say concerns them. And now, turning to the ordinary human beings who are left:

I hope you will not misunderstand what I am going to say. I am not preaching, and Heaven knows I do not pretend to be better than anyone else. I am only trying to call attention to a fact...

What a nifty bit of othering combined not only with the implication that his reader, 'you', was obviously not in that despicable, arrogant out-group, but also with a bit of humble self-deprecation. Marvellous. But he wasn't finished:

" ... I am just the same. That is to say, I do not succeed in keeping the Law of Nature very well, and the moment anyone tells me I am not keeping it, there starts up in my mind a string of excuses as long as your arm.

A neat reinforcement of the idea that he was not pretending to be better than anyone else, with a hint that there was a distinct possibility that he might even be worse. On page 32, he indulged in what was perhaps, at the time, some slightly risqué chumminess:

" I cannot myself see why these things should be the conductors of the new kind of life. But then, if one did not happen to know, I should never have seen any connection between a particular physical pleasure and the appearance of a new human being in the world.

He reiterated his "same as you-ness" on page 41:

" I am just the same. There are bits in this section that I wanted to leave out.

And again on page 53:

" And half of you already want to ask me, "I wonder how you'd feel about forgiving the Gestapo if you were a Pole or a Jew?" ... So do I: I wonder very much.

And once more on page 83:

" I feel a strong desire to tell you - and I expect you feel a strong desire to tell me - which of these two errors is the worse.

Now you and I know that the word 'we' can be inclusive or exclusive, depending on the context in which it is used.
"Hey! Did you forget we are going to the cinema? Stop reading A Maze In Greece and get yourself ready!"
"We are going to the cinema, but you must stay at

home and read A Maze In Greece from cover to cover."

Lewis did use the word 'we' 733 times in Mere Christianity, and a proportion of those uses were of the inclusive type, that is, inclusive of 'you' the reader. I'm too lazy to go through them all to identify how many of the total were inclusive uses of 'we', but here's a token example:

❝ The ordinary idea which we all have before we become Christians is this. (p86)

Quite a clever use of the inclusive 'we', tying it to 'all' in the first instance and, in the second, merely implying an 'all'. Lewis also used "you and I", an explicitly inclusive version of 'we' with an almost conspiratorial feel to it. He employed it quite a few times:

❝ They tell you how the demands of this law, which **you and I** cannot meet ... (p19)

❝ **You and I** can go through this process ... (p31)

❝ I do not suppose **you and I** would ... (p33)

❝ ... be doing more than **you and I** would do if ... (p43)

❝ The reason why I must is that **you and I** ... (p46)

❝ I do not say **you and I** are individually responsible ... (p46)

❝ That is why the little decisions **you and I** make ... (p60)

❝ ... feelings **you and I** are likely to get ... (p69)

❝ And of course **you and I** tend to take it for granted ... (p75)

" He knows what **you and I** are going to do ... (p76)

" **You and I** are concerned with the way things work now. (p79)

" Whereas **you and I** know ... (p98)

" But **you and I** know that ... (p99)

" ... all the different men that **you and I** were intended to be. (p99)

You and I know that "you and I" implies that you and I are a bit special, in an exclusive club of some sort, that we are definitely in agreement, and to disagree would be verging on an act of malice. Not that I would try to coerce you into agreement or anything like that of course.

Regardless of how serious or complicated his subject matter, Lewis employed a casual style for the most part. This was a deliberate choice which he commented on in the Preface:

" In this edition I have expanded the contractions and replaced most of the italics by recasting the sentences in which they occurred: but without altering, I hope, the "popular" or "familiar" tone which I had all along intended.

He didn't say why he'd decided to adopt a 'popular' or 'familiar' tone, but taking into account that it was originally a radio broadcast aimed at 'ordinary' people, perhaps he was trying to avoid "talking over their heads", and thus losing their attention. Nevertheless, his decision to maintain that style in the book indicates he was aware that such a style could aid in getting his message across.

It might seem as if I've been making mountains out of molehills in this chapter, but that's actually the point. A mountain is obvious to everyone, and takes conscious effort to negotiate, whereas molehills are much more easily negotiated, almost without noticing them. Consequently, enough artificial ones suitably placed and camouflaged will subtly guide you in the desired direction. I've simply been putting flags on some of them to make them more visible.

Another way of thinking of it is crab and sweetcorn soup. The crab and the sweetcorn are the main ingredients but the liquid they are immersed in provides the background flavour. Lewis's Bald Assertions, Arguments from Everybody Knows, and so on, are the crab and sweetcorn while the "old pals" act is the background flavour.

More tasty morsels in the next chapter.

But before you go, there's something else that Lewis did which fits into the theme of this chapter. At the end of Chapter 8 I pointed out some instances where he stated that particular things he was saying were just based on guesswork. Here's the example from page 80:

" But that is guesswork. You and I are concerned with the way things work now.

The implication, of course, is that all the bald assertions he made were not based on guesswork.

Reference Links for Chapter 10

1 Beatles: http://goo.gl/VqKzUF

Chapter 11 • Goosey Goosey Gander, Rhymes With ...

In Mere Christianity there is only one direct and explicit reference to a chapter and verse in the Christian bible, and that is in the Preface on page 6:

" The name Christians was first given at Antioch (Acts 11:26) ...

It struck me as slightly odd that a book about Christianity would contain so few references to the Christian bible. Lewis did make reference to it, but usually in a general sense rather than to specific chapters and verses. For example, he referred to "The story in the Book of Genesis" (p27) and "The Golden Rule of the New Testament" (p39), and made remarks such as "the New Testament hates what it calls 'busybodies'" (p40).

He did get a little more specific a few times, although the references are still somewhat vague. Like this from page 41:

" In the passage where the New Testament says that every one must work, it gives as a reason "in order that he may have something to give to those in need."

But then he also made references which give no indication at all of even an approximate location of the source, such as the one following, also from page 41:

" Charity - giving to the poor - is an essential part of Christian morality: in the frightening parable of the sheep and the goats it seems to be the point on which everything turns.

However, to put these quotes in context, in the entire book he only mentioned the Christian bible eleven times, the New Testament eight times, and the Old Testament twice. He did separately mention Paul twice, and Matthew, Mark, Luke, and John the Baptist once, but most of these references were oblique rather than direct. In particular, the quote above which mentions "the frightening parable" is completely opaque if you are not familiar with the Christian bible.

Despite not making many appeals to the authority of the Christian bible, Lewis appears to have thought that on the occasions when he did refer to it his audience would be more than cursorily familiar with its contents. I'll come back to that, but for now I want to return to the topic of Appeals to Authority - the only full-blown example in this book, so far, being the one I made to the imaginary Brian G. Templeford in Chapter 2. In comparison, this appeal by Lewis on page 39 is almost half-hearted:

> ❝ As Dr. Johnson said, "People need to be reminded more often than they need to be instructed."

Lewis used the word 'authority' ten times in total, the first occurrence being on page 20:

> ❝ They [the Christians] tell you how the demands of this law, which you and I cannot meet, have been met on our behalf, how God Himself becomes a man to save man from the disapproval of God. It is an old story and if you want to go into it you will no doubt consult people who have more authority to talk about it than I have.

It's another example of him playing the "ordinary man", a

theme which was highlighted in Chapter 10. The other nine occurrences of 'authority' can all be found in one paragraph on page 32:

" ... I believe it on His authority. Do not be scared by the word authority. Believing things on authority only means believing them because you have been told them by someone you think trustworthy. Ninety-nine per cent of the things you believe are believed on authority. I believe there is such a place as New York. I have not seen it myself. I could not prove by abstract reasoning that there must be such a place. I believe it because reliable people have told me so. The ordinary man believes in the Solar System, atoms, evolution, and the circulation of the blood on authority - because the scientists say so. Every historical statement in the world is believed on authority. None of us has seen the Norman Conquest or the defeat of the Armada. None of us could prove them by pure logic as you prove a thing in mathematics. We believe them simply because people who did see them have left writings that tell us about them: in fact, on authority. A man who jibbed at authority in other things as some people do in religion would have to be content to know nothing all his life.

I have to say I do not agree with all of that. For one thing, I'd say that the true figure for the things you believe on authority is nearer 86.97452% (but then I did pluck that number out of ~~my~~ nowhere in the same way that Lewis plucked his '99'). I wonder what percentage of people think that plucking numbers out of nowhere, and presenting them as percentages, is an unjustified but common Appeal to the Authority of Mathematics.

I'm beginning to think that Lewis had an unrequited love affair with New York, although I suppose a love affair with any city would necessarily be unrequited. I'm fairly certain that he never did visit New York, and therefore continued to accept its existence on the authority of others throughout his life. But I do know that he married an American lady, Joy Davidman Gresham, quite late in his life. How do I know that? As Lewis pointed out, like many things, it is on the authority of others.

The key word in the previous sentence is 'others'. That is to say that I consulted *several* independent sources[1] which all corroborated those facts (and found none that contradicted them) which justifies accepting those facts "on authority". And the key word in the previous sentence is 'independent'. Had I consulted several, or even hundreds, of people who all got their information from the same source, and no one else, then the justification for accepting those facts "on authority" would be slim.

Lewis was correct when he said that we accept facts on the authority of "the scientists", and the reason we do is because there is more than one of them. But not only that, it's because we know that scientists don't just accept facts on the say so of another scientist - they independently check facts before endorsing them. That's how science works. We are less likely to accept something on the authority of a single scientist whose findings have not been confirmed by others.

History is no different really. The more contemporary accounts there are of an historical event, the more likely we are to accept the information on the basis of such authority. And if those accounts are from diverse, independent sources then the value we place on them as valid authorities is heightened accordingly. But it's not just contemporary accounts which influence our acceptance, there is the physical evidence which supports them.

For example, take the Tudor ship the Mary Rose. According to records, it was built around 1510 during the reign of King Henry VIII, and sank in 1545. For more than 400 years the accounts of the ship's existence were the only 'authority' we had, but in 1971 the wreck was discovered and subsequently raised (in 1982), providing the physical evidence.

Buildings, earthworks, burial grounds, places of worship, and more, all provide evidence to corroborate historical accounts, but of course, the further back in time we look the sparser the accounts get and, likewise, the physical evidence. It also gets harder to differentiate between fact and fiction. For instance, there's general agreement that there was a bloke called George who lived about one thousand seven hundred years ago, and that he was a soldier for a time in the Roman army, but even discounting the plainly fictional encounter between him and a dragon, at least some of his alleged activities are considered fictional by some due to insufficient evidence[2].

Lewis gave his examples of how we believe things on authority to support his statement that "believing things on authority only means believing them because you have been told them by someone you think trustworthy". What his examples actually show is that we believe things on authority not when "some*one*" we think we can trust tells us, but when at least several qualified people tell us, and we are more likely to believe them if they have some evidence to back up what they are saying. Perhaps Lewis saw the flaw and that is why he tacked on the end of the paragraph another sweeping, overblown statement (in an attempt to sweep the flaw under the carpet - along with the pun?):

" A man who jibbed at authority in other things as some people do in religion would have to be content to know nothing all his life.

Not only sweeping and overblown, but also utterly incorrect. Jibbing at authority, that is not just meekly accepting it, is the very thing which has resulted in advances in human knowledge and understanding. Had Benjamin Franklin meekly accepted it on authority that *"the surest remedy against thunder is that which our Holy Mother the Church practises, namely, the ringing of bells when a thunderbolt* [lightning] *impends"*[3] he would not have invented the lightning-rod, an invention which has protected tall buildings, somewhat ironically including churches, from the potentially devastating effects of a lightning strike ever since.

Taken as a whole, Lewis's entire paragraph was an attempt to validate his initial statement that he believed something on "His authority" ('His' in this instance being a reference to Jesus Christ). However, none of his examples made the case for believing something on the authority of what was allegedly said or thought by a figure whose status as a god of any sort is not accepted by the majority of humans, and whose very existence is disputed by some.

Lewis's assertion that he believed things on the authority of Jesus Christ reminds me a bit of the Argument from My-Dad's-a-Policeman, an argument which used to pop up now and again during disagreements in the school playground. Typically, one boy would assert that whatever it was he was saying had been certified as true by his dad, "and my dad's a policeman!"

If anyone suggested he was making it up (because nobody had ever seen his father in a police uniform) then he would say his father was a 'plain clothes' detective, and if anyone wanted to they could ask him, but he, the boy, felt he should warn everyone that his father might not be pleased if they did because he was working undercover. Neat, eh? Just call upon a "super authority" who can't really be questioned.

Despite his pleas that he was only an ordinary layman, Lewis's style of writing in Mere Christianity, in large part because of the numerous bald assertions, comes across as if he himself was an authority. Indeed, many of his readers seem to be of the opinion that he was. Not really surprising when he made statements such as this:

> **❝** And that is how Theology started. People already knew about God in a vague way. Then came a man who claimed to be God; and yet he was not the sort of man you could dismiss as a lunatic. He made them believe Him. They met Him again after they had seen Him killed. And then, after they had been formed into a little society or community, they found God somehow inside them as well: directing them, making them able to do things they could not do before. And when they worked it all out they found they had arrived at the Christian definition of the three-personal God. (p73)

I do declare, dear reader, that I had an urge, which I was barely able to resist, to append the words "and they all lived happily ever after" to the quoted statement just to see if anyone would notice. The part that especially made me think of fairytales was the second sentence where Lewis wrote that "people already knew about God in a vague way". Although he didn't actually specify that they were the ones he was referring to, the people amongst whom the "man who claimed to be God" came were people who had very specific ideas about their god (the not-as-yet-but-soon-to-be-hijacked-as-Christian god). Chabad.org makes it quite plain[4]:

> **"** The Torah contains 613 commandments. Of these, 248 are "positive" commands (do's), and 365 are "negative" commands (don'ts). The precepts form the code of the Jew's daily behavior and his way of life. They help him lead an honest, clean, and healthful life, both in body and in spirit. The precepts are generally divided into two groups: The Jew's duties toward his fellow man, and his duties toward his Creator, God.

How specific were the commands? Here's information about the fifth precept[5]:

> **"** The fifth precept is found in the verse, "Let the waters bring forth abundantly the moving (crawling) creatures that have life" (Beresheet 1:20). This verse contains three precepts. The first is to study the Torah; the second is to beget children: and the third is to circumcise a male child on the eighth day of life and remove the foreskin. It is necessary to study the Torah with great effort at all times, in order to amend one's spirit and soul.

Slicing off body parts because they believed their god had commanded it doesn't suggest to me that those people "knew about God in a vague way". That single precept is enough evidence to refute such a statement even without the more than six hundred others. In my book, if I included a statement like Lewis's to support one of my arguments then I would consider myself guilty of lying.

As an aside, did you notice that both those paragraphs about the Torah are male-centric? And despite the mention of foreskins in the second, it is the first which is more so; "*his* way of life", "help *him* lead", "*his* fellow *man*", "*his* duties", "*his* Creator". It seems that Lewis, despite dismissing it as 'vague', had a legacy on which to build his vision.

Is it fair to accuse Lewis of lying when he wrote that "people already knew about God in a vague way"? Is there any evidence to support such an allegation? It probably depends on whether one includes misrepresentation in the lying category. One thing is definite though; he had previously written about those very same people, on page 27, where he had this to say:

" He ['God'] selected one particular people and spent several centuries hammering into their heads the sort of God He was - that there was only one of Him and that He cared about right conduct. Those people were the Jews, and the Old Testament gives an account of the hammering process.

Try as I might, I cannot find a way to interpret those words in any way which suggests vagueness. Hammers have a tendency to make people take notice when they are hit with them, even in a metaphorical sense. But let's be charitable and admit the possibility that in his assertion that they "already knew about God in a vague way" Lewis unwittingly dipped his toes in the sludge at the edges of the hypocritical pool which has come to be known as "Lying for Jesus"[6].

However, putting charity briefly to one side, what

would it mean if Lewis was completely aware of what he was doing with the manipulations and distortions we've been looking at? The content of Mere Christianity, via the original radio broadcasts and especially via the later book, has in effect been repeated many thousands of times, which brings to mind the famous words of Joseph Goebbels, the arch propagandist of the Nazi regime:

" If you repeat a lie often enough, people will believe it, and you will even come to believe it yourself.

What makes that quote so very apposite is that its widespread acceptance as having been said by Goebbels came about by its repeated attribution to him, despite the fact that no reliable source has ever been located to verify he ever said those words (or any of the slight variations which abound)[7], neatly proving its message to be true regardless of where it actually came from.

On page 72, where he was writing about the nature of the Christian god, Lewis wrote:

" ... what God the Father begets is God, something of the same kind as Himself. In that way it is like a human father begetting a human son. But not quite like it. So I must try to explain a little more.

Notice how he allowed himself a modifier in the form of, "but not quite like it". Further down the page he wrote about people who "think that after this life, or perhaps after several lives, human souls will be 'absorbed' into God". According to Lewis:

" They say it is like a drop of water slipping into the sea. But of course that is the end of the drop. If that is what happens to us, then being absorbed is the same as ceasing to exist.

Lewis chose not to afford 'them' the luxury of a "but not quite like it" modifier, preferring to take what "they say" at face value, in order to perfunctorily dismiss it. But even then there's a problem with his dismissal. It is plainly not "the end of the drop" or "the same as ceasing to exist". The atoms and molecules of that drop of water continue to exist, mingling with those already in the sea.

Was Lewis aware of atoms and molecules? Indeed he was. He referred explicitly to molecules on page 14, and to atoms on five other occasions, some of which have been quoted previously in this book. If this was the only instance, or one of very few, where Lewis used questionable methods to advance his agenda, then it would be reasonable to exclaim, "Mr. Lewis! What a naughty boy you were!" However, as we have discovered in the chapters of this book, this latest example was not an isolated occurrence. Throughout Mere Christianity there are multiple occurrences ranging from disingenuous reasoning to outright trickery.

The title of this chapter refers to the old children's nursery rhyme which has its origins in 16th or 17th century England, during a period when Catholics were being given a very hard time by Protestants. For those of you who are not familiar with it, here is a common version of it:

> Goosey Goosey Gander where shall I wander,
> Upstairs, downstairs and in my lady's chamber,
> There I met an old man who wouldn't say his prayers,
> I took him by the left leg and threw him down the stairs.

It is said[8] that the rhyme (and others of a similar nature) was a means of disseminating a message in an age before the written word was widely available or even understood. Accounts suggest various connotations for the 'goose', but it is generally agreed that the second line refers to the location of a small hidden room, often located within the private quarters of well-to-do families, where a Catholic priest could hide from Protestant 'investigators'. The "old man who wouldn't say his prayers" referred to just such a Catholic priest who, being Catholic, refused to say prayers in anything but Latin, contrary to the dictates of the Protestant regime who insisted prayers should be said in English. Apparently "left leg" was a derogatory term for a Catholic, and the throwing down the stairs alluded to the captured priest being put to death.

Communications had advanced somewhat when Lewis decided to make his contribution to the world via Mere Christianity, not only in respect of the channels available, but also in the size of the audience one could hope to address. Radio, and later the relatively cheap and widely available book, allowed Lewis to introduce the masses to the art of sophistry, or more bluntly, the techniques of propaganda. Sadly, rather than teach them *about* sophistry and propaganda, it's clear he chose to use it *on* them.

'Propaganda' is an emotive word, and you might be thinking that it's rather extreme to label what Lewis wrote in that way. And perhaps you would be right if the label was applied in blanket fashion, but there is no mistaking that some elements of propaganda appear in Mere Christianity. For example, Lewis emphasised his 'ordinariness', something which is an aspect of propaganda according to the Changing Minds website[9]:

** Appearing ordinary also makes you appear

134

uncomplicated and very unlikely to tell lies. As a result, people are more likely to trust you further and believe more of what you say.

'Card-stacking' is another aspect, where deliberate action is taken to bias an argument, like in the drop of water example above. However, perhaps the most propaganda-like thing about Mere Christianity is its employment of the "big lie" technique. It will probably be more apparent to someone who is not convinced of the existence of gods, and more so to someone who is convinced of their non-existence, but the book's premise that there is a "Real Morality", that it comes from a creator god which is male and has always existed, who is a being made up of three persons, one of which showed up in 'meatspace' for a while for the purpose of saving its inhabitants from eternal torture, and so on, certainly falls within the BIG category. Whether it's actually a lie is for you to decide, but there is no denying it is BIG, and also that the techniques Lewis used to convince his audience of its truth were sometimes, quite often perhaps, less than full of integrity. How much less I will leave for you to ponder.

One thing seems clear: Mere Christianity was written for people who are predisposed to accept the idea of gods as more than imaginary entities, and for people who are struggling to maintain their faith in the existence of the Christian god. Lewis spoke directly to the latter category when he wrote on page 62:

> **“** There is no need to be worried by facetious people who try to make the Christian hope of "Heaven" ridiculous by saying they do not want "to spend eternity playing harps." The answer to such people is that if they cannot understand books written for grown-ups, they

should not talk about them.

And a very grown-up answer it would be too if nobody ever got past the age of twelve, but then Lewis certainly knew how to feed his allies' egos by denigrating his, and by implication their, enemies.

In this book I have given numerous examples where Lewis used techniques to manipulate and even hoodwink his audience. There are more I didn't mention, just waiting to be discovered by you. But beware. Lewis was a clever person so you need to stay alert, especially if you fall into one of the categories mentioned above for whom, I believe, Mere Christianity was written.

To close, I will leave you with an aphorism I've seen floating about the online social networks:

Knowledge is having the right answer
Intelligence is asking the right question

"When is a maze not a maze?" is not the right question, any more than "when it's amazing" is the right answer.

What's your next question?

Reference Links for Chapter 11

1 Lewis's marriage: http://goo.gl/eRgzpq

2 Saint George: http://goo.gl/JnNRrc

3 Franklin's rod: http://goo.gl/IXcM6U

4 Torah commandments: http://goo.gl/axC9Zx

5 Torah precepts: http://goo.gl/TYPihH

6 Lying for Jesus: http://goo.gl/LUfrAX

7 'Goebbels' quote: http://goo.gl/ravis6

8 Goosey gander: http://goo.gl/VXU4ms

9 'Ordinary' propaganda: http://goo.gl/JYDynV

Chapter 12 • A Bonus Chapter

Everybody likes a bonus, don't they? If you are one of those mean spirited people who don't appreciate an offer made in good faith then I suggest you leave now - this chapter is not for you!

But enough of my silly WWLS games. The reason this is a bonus chapter is that it is not about Lewis's writing in Mere Christianity. While it seems unlikely that anyone who might react with, "well thank Christ for that!" would still be reading this far into the book, perhaps having found an excuse to cast it aside when they spied an error or fallacy in my writing, if you are such a person then stick around. This chapter is about just that. Yes folks, this is the chapter which exposes the underhand techniques I used in this book to get you where I want you.

And, you might well be wondering, where exactly is that?

In my pocket?

Under my thumb?

At my mercy?

An unwitting puppet in my drive for world domination?

...Time for a quick (and dirty) "bwahahaha!" methinks.

Wouldn't you know it, while writing this book my plans for world domination were nowhere to be found so I just had to make do with passing on my observations about some of the ways in which people try to manipulate the thoughts of others. I am, of course, grateful to Mr Lewis for providing such wonderful examples, but there were many others who tried to manipulate my thoughts over the years. Sometimes they were successful (and probably some still are, at least to some degree), but time, and the lessons learnt, have made me less gullible. And that's where I want you to be. To be less gullible.

Gullible!? That's insulting, right? Who do I think I am calling you gullible!!?

And the answer is: I'm not calling you gullible in a calling-you-names sort of way. You might well be less gullible than I am (on some as yet undiscovered absolute and universal scale of gullibleness). But are we not all gullible to some extent about some things some of the time? Is there anyone who could truly say they have never been gullible about anything? I certainly can't. And that's why being *less* gullible is usually an achievable goal..

But how about we turn it around and think about the way we try to persuade people to our own point of view. How many of us use manipulative techniques in our communications with others, making use of any gullibility we notice in them? Do we do it wittingly or unwittingly? Do you?

Relatively few of the 'ordinary' people I've crossed paths with wittingly use manipulative techniques, but nevertheless 'ordinary' people do use them. We learn them from an early age, from the time we become self-aware, from the time that we begin to notice that our behaviour and how we express ourselves affects how people respond to us. We learn to tune our communications. We learn it from our parents, our siblings and extended family if we have them, and the growing number of people who come within our compass, until it becomes second nature.

Unless you choose not to communicate at all, it is obviously necessary to choose the words you use, the form in which you string them together, and the style in which you present them. The English language, and I'm sure most if not all languages, provides multitudinous options when it comes to choosing words, even ~~simple~~ ~~basic~~ ~~fundamental~~ ~~uncomplicated~~ straightforward ones. And the way you put words together, the form in which you structure them, is also open to extensive variation. Short and sweet, or verbosely and painstakingly step-by-step in long-winded fashion from start to finish, are just two of many presentation styles. Quite often our choices bubble out of us without much prior deliberation.

There was a time when I would have said, almost without thinking, that I *confess* that where I want you to be is in two places at once: *less* gullible, and *more* aware of how you tune your part in a conversation. I hope it is an indication that I have been at least partially successful in understanding past manipulations by others that I now choose to *declare* it rather than confess - a declaration of independence of sorts.

If I've been successful in getting you where I want you, or you were already there without any help from me (thanks very much!), then a chapter by chapter run down of how I attempted to manipulate your thoughts should be unnecessary - you'll already be aware of my nefarious doings. However, as my homage to transparency, I'll highlight some of them anyway.

Chapter 1 was actually pretty straightforward - the maze story was the bait on the hook to get you interested and turning pages which, as you are still reading, appears to have worked. And having commented on Lewis's "old pals" act, it seems noteworthy to point out that I went further than he did, taking the risk of engaging you directly in a down-to-earth style, with 'asides' and direct questions. Did you find it engaging?

Throughout the book I adopted an irreverent attitude towards what Lewis wrote, designed to establish that I am not anything like the "stuffed shirt" he often came across as. Stuffed shirt? Nope. Not me. I'm a guy with a modicum of street cred - I wrote "Wut!?" in Chapter 2.

Although I'm outing some of my techniques in this chapter, I actually made use of the self-exposure technique to gain your trust earlier in the book. In Chapter 2, for example, where I revealed my invention of Brian G Templeford. And again in Chapter 9 with the Gandhi/Hitler quotes.

I got quite busy in Chapter 3, using humour to denigrate ("Does a person need a capital P ...?"), going on to use the Argument from He Said She Said after implying I wasn't going to, side-stepping the question about forgiveness via the imaginary sunset, and used an innuendo laden phrase - "I'll leave it to you to check out if he used one or two hands on those occasions" - as part of my ongoing background 'assault' on dear old Clive (for those who don't know, Mr Lewis's initials stood for Clive Staples, and as a bonus fact in a bonus chapter, I'll tell you his nickname was Jack).

Wherever I used the Argument from He Said She Said, I always put the 'good' words in your mouth, not mine. And what about all those bald assertions? Boy do I have a cheek! Then there was the final sentence of Chapter 9 which I used to reinforce my allegations but didn't deliver on the promises in the next chapter. And how about the time I used "You and I know" before I'd written about the use of "you and I" as a device?

There are plenty more examples littered throughout this book, but I'll leave it as an exercise (if you want to take it on) to re-read it with a critical eye to find them. However, there is one thing I want to pick up on. In Chapter 9 I said I would come back to the question "Can 'evil' people love?" and that's what I want to address now.

When we think about 'classically' evil people, Hitler regularly appears on people's lists, and would be a contender for the number one slot on many. His activities as Führer are well documented, and the atrocities committed under his leadership were ultimately his responsibility, leading many people to consider him evil through and through. If anyone is a candidate for occupancy of the pit of evil, the part beyond the point of no return on the 'good ↔ evil' scale illustrated in Chapter 9, then Hitler is it.

In Chapter 3 I mentioned my dog Willie, and that I know he not only forgives me but loves me too. What I didn't mention is that it is reciprocal. Despite the fact that I feel compelled to administer a rebuke when he forgets the rules, I too forgive and love him. It's easy to tell, you only have to look at the way he nuzzles up to me and how I stroke and pet him.

There is a video clip of a man showing love for his dog (which you can download from http://goo.gl/bQNWZW). In the video, the man is petting the dog, including rubbing faces together, in a display of affection. The dog's name was Blondi, and, as it happens, the man caressing her was that Hitler bloke. It can be jarring to the mind trying to reconcile the 'evil' status of Hitler with his obvious affection for his dog, a state called cognitive dissonance if I've understood the term correctly, and there is more than one way to deal with it.

One way is to entirely dismiss the unwanted conflicting item by declaring that it is not what it appears to be. In the case of Hitler, we have already decided he was evil through and through because there is a mountain of evidence showing his 'evil' nature, and consequently we have placed him in the pit of evil at the far right of our scale. Obviously the show of affection for a few seconds in a video was just put on for the camera, or he was fooling the dog so that he could enjoy killing her shortly before he took his own life, or ..., or ....

Another option is to examine the model we are using, our 'good ↔ evil' scale, to see if it is an accurate depiction of what it is designed to represent. Clearly it doesn't cater for people who are recognisably in the evil category who also have non-evil, 'good' aspects to their character. Rather than try to massage the data to fit our model, we could change the model to more accurately reflect the data.

You'd think that the second option is obviously better than the first, but observation of how people actually behave reveals it is apparently not considered to be so. In fact it appears that a significant number of people choose neither of those options, preferring to metaphorically walk away and look at something easier to deal with (like TV, or any of the more modern forms of 'entertainment'). When it comes down to it, the people who go for the second option seem to be in the minority, the remainder dogmatically clinging to the models they are attached to, by explaining away the shortcomings.

The problem with the linear 'good ↔ evil' scale, even in the two-dimensional version in Chapter 9, is that it is based on an either-or premise. To left of centre you are 'good', to the right you are 'bad'. But people are not like that. People do both 'good' and 'bad' things, and it's the proportion of one to the other which determines how 'good' or 'bad' they are. We need a scale which can reflect that.

And, as luck would have it, there is one. Think of the Scales of Justice held by the Lady of Justice on top of The Old Bailey (The Central Criminal Court in London). It is a balance scale, and the idea of it can be used to represent the proportion of 'good' and 'bad' in a person in a more realistic way.

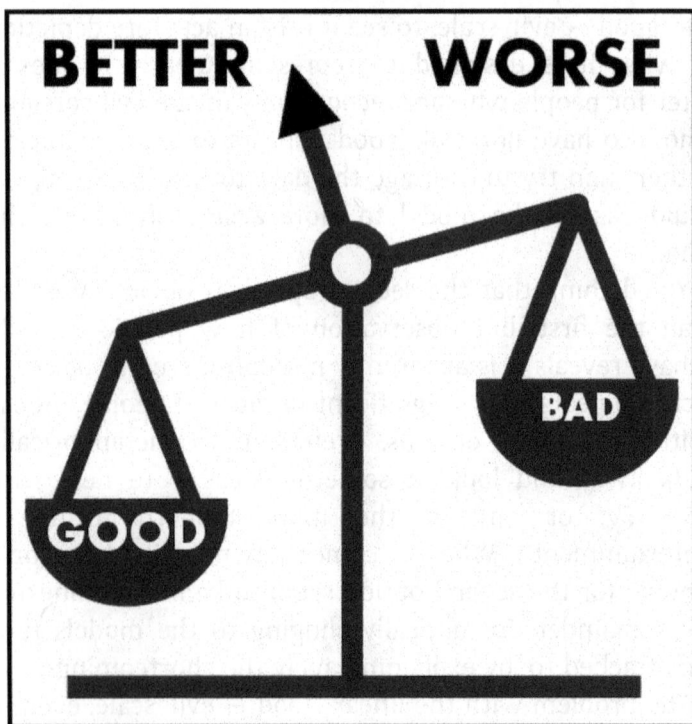

Although it doesn't feature a pit of evil, which some

might think a diabolical omission, it's a much more dynamic representation of a person who occupies the spot where I put you and I on the linear scale in Chapter 9. Indeed there is no need for a pit of evil because this model caters for any amount of 'good' and any amount of 'bad' in any combination, adjusting the pointer accordingly. It shows that no matter how many "units of bad" there might be within a person, the "units of good" will counteract them. Of course the same holds true for the reverse, but nevertheless this model shows that nobody is irredeemably bad'. And if I have persuaded you to my way of thinking, then perhaps I have also demonstrated the power of infographics. Just one more weapon in the arsenal of the dedicated manipulator.

Which brings me to the final topic in this book: the morality of manipulation. We have observed many examples of manipulative techniques, some which appear in Mere Christianity and then, in this chapter, some which appear in this book. Dictionary definitions reveal that the word manipulation is generally associated with the less-than-respectable activity of exerting shrewd or devious influence, especially for one's own advantage. But what about exerting shrewd or devious influence to bestow advantage on others? Is manipulation morally justifiable if it's purpose is to benefit others?

"Danger, Will Robinson!"[2]

That road takes us perilously close to "the end justifies the means" territory. The end justifies the means is arguably true in some rare, emergency circumstances, but manipulation is not an emergency technique. The morality of manipulation is not defined by its purpose, but by its nature. If it is based on a falsehood, or a fallacy, and the person doing the manipulating is aware of it (and never reveals that fact), then the manipulation is immoral by my standards of morality.

Going a step further, if the types of manipulation used to support and promote it are immoral, what does that say about the morality of whatever it is which is being promoted? It doesn't necessarily follow that it too is immoral - the manipulator might be acting in an unauthorised capacity for her or his own benefit. However, if an unauthorised manipulator who is acting for his or her own benefit goes unchallenged by authorised representatives of whatever is being promoted, it justifiably casts doubt on its morality. Organisations which further their aims and agendas by directly employing, or otherwise making use of, people who can legitimately be called authorised manipulators, are altogether a different kettle of rotting fish, the putrid odour of corruption spilling forth.

Manipulative techniques are in constant use all around us, most obviously in commercial advertising, much of which falls into that category of manipulation known as persuasion. Advertising watchdogs are tasked with separating what is acceptable persuasion from what is unacceptable manipulation, and some of them have statutory powers to insist that advertisers adhere to the prescribed standards.

I don't know if it is unique to the Philippines, nor even if there is an advertising watchdog there, but TV adverts which include claims of 'health' benefits appear to be required to display and speak the words "No approved therapeutic claims" at some point. Observation reveals that the point chosen is invariably right at the end of the advert (after making copious use of the aforementioned manipulative techniques to promote the product's efficacy and 'natural goodness' or whatever), at which point the message is flashed briefly on screen while someone with the ability to speak amazingly fast utters the words of the message. Manipulation at its finest.

There is no shortage of material in which to search out examples of manipulative techniques in action. Some of them are relatively benign, others not so much. Some of those 'others' might result in a wallet or purse which is less full than it might be, or worse, a case of indebtedness which, for some, will become a severe burden. Worse still, a proportion of those 'others' will shackle a person's mind, restricting their ability to use it. My parting shot, for what it's worth is this:

> Sometimes it is possible to break open a shackle
> Sometimes it has to be picked open over time
> But in every case
> The first thing which needs to be done
> Is to discover the existence of the shackle

And finally, inspired by the thought that some readers might still be grumbling (or worse) about the omission of 'evil' from the revised 'good ↔ evil' scale, here's a farewell gift designed to fill an idle moment (such moments being the target of the horn-ed one, or so I was led to believe). There are, and have been for many years, cartoon drawings which appear under the "Love is..." banner[3]. You may have seen them in newspapers and elsewhere. There have been thousands of them, which is perhaps testimony to the amorphous nature of love and the difficulty of precisely defining it.

You have probably guessed it already, but my farewell gift is a twist on the "Love is..." idea. You simply have to complete the following sentence:

"Evil is..."

Here's one to get the ball rolling...

Evil is...

...perpetuating your fears through your child

And that's not funny.
I'm sure you can do much better than that.
Fear is a venomous emotion, and laughter is the antidote.

Notes and Reference Links for Chapter 12

1 The more astute (or possibly anal retentive?) may have observed that the model does not in fact show that nobody is irredeemable. If enough "units of bad" are in the right-hand container then the balance bar will adopt an exactly vertical position, and, once in that position, adding "units of good" to the other container will have no effect (unless an external force is applied to the balance bar). Models don't necessarily have to be perfect to be useful illustrations, but nevertheless I'm sure someone, somewhere, will be able to find something in their pot of woo (something 'quantum' perhaps?) to conjure up the mysterious external force.

2 Lost in Space: http://goo.gl/cpaSjy

3 Love is: http://goo.gl/VF3wQj

Postface

I considered putting at least some of what I'll write here in a more traditional Preface at the beginning of the book. Lewis included a Preface in the edition of Mere Christianity I read in which, amongst other things, he attempted to address various criticisms, and to explain why he'd made changes. Other authors use a Preface to put their book in some kind of context. I came to the conclusion that if I didn't achieve what I set out to achieve with this book without a prior explanation, then I had failed.

All the same, having read it (you have read it, right? If you haven't then get out of here right now and go read it), and hopefully having got[1] something out of it, you might be interested to know a bit more about the author. If not, then thanks for reading, and bye for now.

So, who am I? Well, I am an ordinary bloke who happens to like reading and writing. In Chapter 10 I noted that Lewis took some pains to convey a sense that he was "just like you", "ordinary", "one of the common people", despite his academic prowess. I have no such conflict to deal with. My mediocre academic achievements mark me quite unequivocally an ordinary man. And that is the reason I am revealing this information here rather than in a Preface. Like it or not, I suspect that knowledge of my (lack of) 'credentials' prior to reading this book might well have a negative influence on a reader's perception of my work. Be that as it may, I have no desire to hide the truth, nor to pretend that it is other than it is. My desire, for what it's worth, is that my work should be taken on its merits rather than judged by what I did or did not achieve in my younger years.

This is not my first book. I previously wrote a semi-autobiographical novel (the default subject matter for many a first book). However, I wrote it under the pen name Jo S. Wun. There's a story behind that which I will share with you here.

Jo S. Wun is the shortened version of the full pen name I invented: Jo Sun Wun. The 'eastern' influence came about for two reasons. One reason was the title of the book: The Jeremy - Snaps of the Dragon. The 'dragon' referred to the fact that I was born in 1952, a year which according to Chinese astrology is somehow associated with dragons. It rather tickled me that my year of birth was claimed to be connected with a mythical beast by a system of pseudo-science, a system which one of the characters in the book makes reference to. I do feel obliged, however, to emphasise that I think the Chinese version of astrology is as bunkumesque as the 'western' version.

The other reason for its 'eastern' feel was that the pen name is actually a joke which is revealed by saying the full name, Jo Sun Wun, out loud while pretending you are Chinese or Japanese. I apologise if you actually are Chinese or Japanese, and beg your forgiveness - it was not my intention to insult you! If you still haven't got it, then this link might help: http://goo.gl/hx7zJS. I hope I don't need to point out that I do not actually have any illusions (or delusions for that matter) about my status in this world - it's just my sense of humour.

But why use a pen name at all?

Good question. However, the answer is not straightforward, and if I was to answer it I would probably find myself floundering in a pool of hindsight bias. Let's just say it seemed like a good idea at the time.

The book is available in printed form from various outlets[2], and as an ebook, in various formats, from the Smashwords website[3].

A word about punctuation and spelling

Punctuation and spelling can get some people into an irate state. That is, of course, if it doesn't comply with the rules which they happen to think are the correct ones. Indeed there are some who appear to think that grammar and spelling are subject to Laws with a capital 'L'. I concede that I have a tendency to get grumpy over omitted or misplaced apostrophes, my favourite aphorism on the subject being "An apostrophe is the difference between knowing your shit and knowing you're shit", but my views on grammar and spelling in general are quite relaxed.

I don't maintain a stock of what-is-the-younger-generation-coming-to soap with which to get in a lather about 'text-speak' and its implications for the future collapse of society. I might make a comment if you write "your an idiot" (about the missing apostrophe, not the slur on my character), but if you write "ur an idiot n i dont lyk ur attitude" I probably won't pass comment at all (because it adheres to the 'rules' of text-speak). The point is that the fundamental purpose of writing is to communicate, to get a message across. But that's a whole subject in itself which would probably be worthy of a book.

In this book I used rules of grammar; the ones which make sense to me. For example, regarding the use of double-quotes, if they are used to indicate direct speech, I include the final punctuation mark (a full stop, period, exclamation point, or whatever) *before* the ending quote mark. However, if they are used to indicate a quote from a written work, or simply to mark something as somehow separate, then I put the final punctuation mark (if any) *after* the ending quote mark.

In regard to spelling, having been educated in England, I tend to use British spellings, but I don't really care if colour is spelt, or spelled, colour or color. I care much more about what is being said than how it is spelt. For instance, despite the fact that it is in common use by at least some of the people it refers to, I find the phrase "people of colour" a tad irksome no matter how it is spelt, probably because it reminds me of the term 'Coloureds', which has bad associations in my mind with the apartheid era in South Africa.

Fanciful Arbitrary Questions

There may be some people who have questions about what my beliefs actually are. Lewis had a penchant for including imaginary people and conversations in his book which seems like a good excuse to include an imaginary FAQ section here.

"Do you believe in God?"
Have you actually read this book?

"So you're an atheist, eh?"
I am a human being who is very much like every other human being, both the dead ones, the ones that are alive, and the ones yet to be born. I care about the lives of all of them, regardless of the

labels they might apply to themselves, or the labels which others apply to them, or any labels others apply to me.

"So you're a humanist, eh?"
I am a human being who recognises the similarities between himself and all the other creatures who have previously inhabited this planet, those that still do, and those that will in the future. I care about their lives too, regardless of what 'station' they occupy in the hierarchy of life.

"So you're an animal lover, eh?"
I am a human being who recognises the importance of all living things, past, present, and future. I also recognise that the continued existence of the 'lower' forms of life depends, in part, upon the choices made by human beings, and yet, those very same 'lower' forms would very likely continue to exist without us. The same cannot be said for humans, who could not exist without many of those 'lower' forms.

"So you're a tree-hugger, eh?"
There are times when hugging a tree would probably be more rewarding than answering fanciful arbitrary questions...

"You must believe in something! What do you believe in?"
Universal human rights will do for a start.

Website/Blog

http://jharps.co.uk

Notes and Reference Links for the Postface

1 I'm contemplating writing a Special Edition for readers who prefer American English. In the meantime, here's a Special Addition: +ten

2 Book availability: http://goo.gl/k4tHdZ

3 Smashwords: http://goo.gl/NusJjG

Acknowledgements

The maze image on the cover was derived from one created at davidbau.com: http://goo.gl/iZki2A

The lettering used on the cover was derived from Quantum Round Hollow BRK, a free font by Brian Kent, using GIMP to create individual graphic image versions of each required letter. The font can be found at most websites which feature free fonts, and a bit about Brian Kent can be found here: http://goo.gl/GJYbgk

GIMP is short for GNU Image Manipulation Program which can be found here: http://www.gimp.org

The image in Chapter 9 was created from scratch using GIMP, and those in Chapter 12 were manipulated in GIMP using images found at: https://openclipart.org

This book was originally authored using the portable version of *Sigil - the EPUB Editor* from PortableApps.com: http://goo.gl/aVstae

This print version was prepared using the portable version of *LibreOffice* from PortableApps.com: http://goo.gl/WUi4Q

The font used for the PDF and print versions of this book is Fontin by Jos Buivenga: http://goo.gl/RMahSv